Bringing Light to Loss is a profound testament to the human spirit's ability to heal and persevere. This book is a gift to anyone seeking comfort, courage, and a renewed sense of purpose. It's a beautiful reminder that even after loss, life still holds meaning, beauty, and hope

Rachael Jayne Groover. Best-selling author of Unshakable Inner Peace

This is a story of resilience, love and hope. Tania inspires us through her powerful stories and at the same time brings the reader through a journey of self-discovery. Her coaching questions and snippets of theories and concepts are purposely woven throughout the book to help us reflect on our own grief and losses, so we can rise up and flourish.

Beverley Patwell, Author Leading Meaningful Change. Capturing the Hearts, Minds and Souls of the People You Lead, Work with and Serve

Bringing Light to Loss is an inspiring and deeply personal reflection of the author's journey of loss, grief, resilience and healing made possible by the unbreakable bond of love. With a passionate writing style and powerful storytelling, Tania brings us a message of hope helping the reader to realize that even in the face of pain and of despondency, we can become empowered to reclaim joy and purpose.

Antonio Bernardelli, Psychologist

There are fast reads, and then there are reads that guide you into a new way of thinking. Tania's emotional journey is evident as we read through the pages of *Bringing Light to Loss*. People talk about starting over. Tania suggests you cannot start over but you can change direction. You can break the cycle. She challenges us with the question; are you willing to try. She succeeds in stirring within the reader new thought processes. A challenge to all.

Iryna Melnyk. Educator B. Sc. , M.A. Comparative Education

TANIA CHOMYK

Bringing light to loss

Redefining grief to reclaim hope and meaning

Published by Deep Pacific Press
117 E 37th St. #580, Loveland, Colorado 80538

Deep
Pacific
Press

DeepPacificPress.com

ISBN 978-1-956108-38-5 (paperback)
ISBN 978-1-956108-39-2 (eBook)

Cover design & illustration: Patrick Knowles

Interior design & formatting: Mark Thomas / Coverness.com

Hope is the thing with feathers that perches in the soul—
and sings the tune without the words—and never stops at all.
                                                    Emily Dickinson

DEDICATED

To my angel, Danylo, whose love remains the heartbeat of my soul. ♥

To my children, who give me reason, hope, and strength to continue.

To all parents navigating the unthinkable—may you find solace in knowing that love transcends all, transforming even the deepest pain into something eternal.

The deeper purpose of this book revealed itself in a quiet moment, not through a word for the year but a vivid image: a red heart followed by a purple heart. The red symbolizes fierce, unconditional love that binds us across generations; the purple reflects loss, courage, and healing. Together, they speak of love's power to endure and transform, even through the greatest loss.

With every beat of my heart, I honor you, Danylo, and the legacy of love and resilience carried by my mother, my grandmother, and all ancestors who bore their stories of heartache and hope. Through this book, I honor them and all who carry the weight of loss with courage, grace, and an unwavering spirit. The hearts of the past continue to guide those who carry them forward.

Proceeds from this book will be donated to the 'Child Life' Program at the Montreal Children's Hospital, in honor of Danylo. Though brief, his legacy will continue to bring smiles and moments of joy to others. The 'Child Life' Program offers vital emotional and developmental support to children and families during their hospital journeys—through music therapy, pet therapy, the comforting presence of "Dr. Clowns," and much more. Their work helps normalize the hospital experience, turning fear and uncertainty into moments of connection and healing. By supporting this cause, you help ensure no child faces illness alone.

May these pages remind you to cherish the hearts in your life, honor the legacy of those who came before, and follow the rhythm of your own heartbeat.

Love endures. Love transforms. Love connects us all.

TABLE OF CONTENTS

INTRODUCTION

The storm came without warning, silent yet devastating. It tore through my life with an intensity I never expected. A mother's worst nightmare. The one thing we try not to imagine when we hold our children close happened to me. And nothing, absolutely nothing, could have prepared me for it.

At the time, I didn't know how to move forward. How could I, when the very fabric of my life had unraveled?

My world felt like a constant storm of confusion, grief, and pain. Yet, deep down, I knew there had to be more to life than just surviving this devastation. This book is for those who find themselves on that island of struggle—that island where loss sets up camp in your soul and you can't imagine how to escape. It's for anyone who feels trapped in the thick of grief, unsure if or how they'll ever find themselves again.

But, as I stand here today reflecting on that pain, I can say that I've learned something powerful: we have the ability to choose how we move forward, even when life forces us to face our worst fears. You do not heal by ignoring your pain or acting like it didn't happen. True healing comes from facing your grief, learning from it, and growing stronger because of what you've been through. This journey is about accepting our pain, embracing it, and finding the way to peace and freedom, just as I did.

This book is not just about my story, but about the legacy of strength and resilience passed down through three generations of women. It's about the collective wisdom that lives within all of us, reminding us that even in the darkest of times, we can choose how to react to the storms of life. With every hardship we face, we are given an opportunity to rise again, just as my great-grandmother, grandmother, and mother did before me. Together, we'll explore how to navigate grief, unlock the power within, and, most importantly, live with gratitude—despite the pain.

I invite you to walk with me through this process. Whether you've experienced loss or are seeking to break free from the patterns that hold you back, know this: healing is not only possible, it is your birthright. And the greatest gift you can give yourself is the chance to heal, to grow, and to live fully, despite the pain.

MILLION-DOLLAR FAMILY

Shattering Dreams, Embracing Healing

UNPREPARED

Twenty-five years ago

*Loss binds us together as human beings; grief is a part of life that
we will experience sooner or later, whether it takes the form of death,
a relationship, a career, or our hopes and dreams.*

Anonymous

When I was a little girl, my mother would say, "Tania, if you are going to have children, think of having at least two so neither will ever be alone."

I had every mother's dream. First, I had a girl, and then I had a boy. I had the perfect family. They call that 'the million-dollar family'.

I had it all.

It was 5:30 in the morning when I opened my eyes and whispered to my husband in surprise, "What an angel! He slept through the night."

Little did I know that the true meaning of this otherwise common expression would be realized that morning, November 11, 1998, when our baby Danylo, at the tender age of six months, was taken from us to join the angels in heaven.

Although he didn't cry out as he normally did when he woke, I entered his room just the same. A strange eeriness washed over me as I approached his crib. Not a single movement. Not a sound. Did my eyes deceive me? Was there a faint blue hue on his left cheek, or was it just the reflection of the streetlights? It couldn't be. The moment my hand touched his body, a coldness unlike anything I'd ever felt took over me. Hysterical, I screamed, and it seemed as though the sound would never really stop. I desperately picked him up and wrapped him in his blanket, wanting to keep him warm as I frantically tried to resuscitate him. But my husband knew our son had left us hours ago. My screams and cries filled the room with desperate pleas and questions. "Oh my God, this can't be happening!" "My baby can't be dead!" "What did I do?"

But no matter how much I cried, or how much I screamed, nothing could bring him back.

Our daughter Larissa shot out of her bed, her face streaked with tears, unable to grasp the gravity of what was happening. She saw me holding Danylo's lifeless body, my voice frantic as I screamed at the 911 operator. I held our son close, rocking back and forth, numb, frozen in disbelief. This can't be happening!

The chaos that followed was overwhelming—police, forensics, and family flooded the house, their shock filling the air. The loud voices, the noise, and the presence of so many strangers made it feel as though my home had been overtaken, as if I were a prisoner in my own grief. But through it all, I kept rocking Danylo, whispering to him, "I'm here. I won't leave you. I will always be here for you. I promise."

I was frozen in time. Hours passed and then the moment arrived when I had no choice but to hand Danylo over to these strangers. Would this be the last time I'd see his beautiful face, his dark hair and eyes? Would I never again hear his sweet voice or see his smile? Would this be the last time I'd feel his soft skin pressed against mine, or hear him splash and laugh in the warm bath water that always made me smile? This could not be happening. No! No! No!

When the police officer gently approached, opening his arms to take Danylo, I was trembling. I simply could not bear to let him go.

Where would he go? Who would care for him?

When I finally handed Danylo over, it felt as though not just my baby was taken from me, but part of my very soul left with him…forever.

Children are not supposed to die before their parents. THEN WHY?

How can this be happening? This must be a bad dream, a horrifying nightmare! If I can just fall asleep and wake up again, maybe it will all go away.

I so desperately wanted it to be a nightmare. I could handle a horrific nightmare. But this...this wasn't the kind of nightmare you wake up from.

I felt utterly helpless, angry, and overwhelmed with a guilt that weighed so heavily on me. How could I have not protected him? Why didn't I check on him again before I went to sleep? Or maybe I did? Maybe I did and just didn't notice anything. Thoughts and images replayed in my mind over and over again—especially the image of him lying on his stomach. It didn't help when I was reminded by his father that, as the child's mother, I should have checked on him.

For a while I lost all motivation to continue with daily life. I became isolated, detached from family, friends, and the world around me. And most of all, I became detached from myself. The only person who kept me going, who kept me smiling, who gave me a reason to keep moving forward, was my daughter Larissa.

In the moments when I was left alone with my thoughts, I yearned to have Danylo back. I longed to undo everything, to clear my sins, to rewind time and make everything right—just as it was before. I questioned God, asking how He could allow this to happen, how could he take our child away? What did I do? Was I being punished for my sins? This was my fault.

The rage and resentment I felt toward anyone I thought could have prevented this—his doctors, the hospital, and even God—was overwhelming. My anger was like nothing I had ever experienced before, and I have never felt it so intensely since.

I felt so incredibly lonely. I wanted another chance to care for him—to comfort him, to clean him, to touch him, to bathe him, to make him laugh, to hear the babbling sounds that would have eventually turned into words. Would his first word have been *Mama*?

I would never know.

If only I could go back in time. If only I had gone to him late at night. If only I could have prevented it. If only, if only, if only…

The autopsy revealed that Danylo died of natural causes. They concluded that his heart had palpitated too much for his body to sustain, and it just stopped. His beautiful little six-month-old body, the one I had held in my arm's countless times, stopped breathing. Why? How could this happen? He passed away peacefully in his sleep, no pain, no struggle. It was as though he had become the purest angel of God.

That was what I had to accept. It was as it was meant to be…even if it made no sense to me. There was nothing I could have done to change it. Nothing.

After the funeral, the house was filled with people—family and friends. I knew they were there because I could hear their voices, but was I? I felt completely oblivious to their presence. I didn't want to talk to anyone. I couldn't answer any questions. I felt emotionless, hollow—as though I was physically present but somehow far, far away.

If only I could have him back. Maybe he's here, and this is just a bad dream.

My ears heard the chatter, but my mind was shrouded in a cloud of fog, distant and numb.

Time passed, and the house grew quieter. Every day, after walking Larissa to school, I'd enter Danylo's room, glance around, and sit in the rocking chair. I realized that rocking had been something I had done since childhood. There was comfort in the motion, especially with some background music. It might also explain why I always found peace on the swings at the park. Later, in our second home, we had a glider in the beautifully maintained backyard where I would escape with my books and coffee. I could spend hours outside, watching the children play and swim, gently gliding back and forth. They'd always know where to find me and would make their way over when it was snack time or when they needed a break from the water. It was my peaceful escape.

This motion, the rocking, was my way of dealing with distress, of comforting myself. I would hold Danylo's favorite blanket close to my face, trying desperately to keep his scent alive. The soft, mild baby scent that was so fresh, so pure, so distinctly him. The leaves had changed colours and were swirling on the ground, marking the end of a season. Weeks passed and slowly I began to piece together my broken world. Or at least, I tried.

I clung to his blanket for as long as I could, just to breathe in his scent. It was all I had left. His favorite toys, his high-chair, bassinette, and car seat, his swing and playpen…they were all empty. The house was eerily quiet.

This wasn't supposed to happen. His last cardiologist appointment went well. The lesions in his heart were closing. The murmur was controlled. "It's insignificant," the cardiologist had said. "We'll see you in six months for a follow-up."

Then WHY?

"You have to accept it, Tania, and go on. You know he wasn't one hundred percent healthy. It could have been worse—Danylo could have suffered later. You have Larissa. You need to be strong for her."

What?! How could my mother speak to me like this?

So, what if he had a few lesions in his heart? They were closing. So, what if one of his kidneys wasn't developed? Who says it would not over time? And, so what if he was missing a piece of his corpus callosum? For all I knew, maybe I was missing mine too!

My mother's words felt so cold, so distant, so unaware of my pain. They had cut through me, and she had no idea how much they stung. Yet, strangely, they were true.

Still, I resented her for saying them so I kept my distance. I realized later that she hadn't known what to say or do. She did the best she could with what she knew. But, at the time, I was lost in my sorrow, and her words didn't comfort me. They may have been the very words I needed to hear because she saw how much I was suffering, but neither she nor anyone else could truly understand what I was going through…until one day, unfortunately, she did.

Reflecting on my pregnancy with Danylo, it was different. For one, I did not gain weight like I did when I was pregnant with my daughter Larissa— twenty-five kilograms (fifty-five pounds). Can you believe that? I felt like a beached whale. Sure, it was a summer delivery…but really? I retained so much water that my shoe size went from a seven to a nine. Imagine that! I didn't recognize myself in pictures, especially at my baby shower: *Who was that huge redhead?*

In December 1997, I had my first ultrasound. I lay quietly on the table with the radiologist scanning my stomach. There seemed to be a long period of silence. It's not in my nature to panic, so I didn't…but I found the silence to be long. The doctor came in and told me that they noticed something in my baby's brain. That caught me off guard. "What? What do you mean?"

I was told that it seemed like one of his ventricles was not fully dilated. That meant he may need a shunt at birth to create room for blood to pass through his brain. This couldn't be certain until he would be born.

Wow! Not exactly what I expected to hear from the ultrasound. Did it scare me? Yes. Did I let it consume me? No.

I was a little nervous but then I thought to myself: *Everything will be okay. It's in God's hands. I won't let this worry me and affect the rest of my pregnancy. Danylo will be fine. We will welcome him into this world with open arms and make sure he has everything he needs to be healthy.*

I wonder, was that the beginning of his fate?

On May 22, 1998, our beautiful son Danylo was born weighing eight pounds, fifteen ounces. Because his ultrasounds had raised some health concerns, Danylo was thoroughly examined. His platelets were low but it appeared the issue with the ventricles in his brain was no longer prevalent. Yay!

Instead, they found that a piece of his corpus callosum was missing. They did not seem to think much of it but wanted me to monitor his development at home. We were told that it could be hereditary, but unless we, his parents, got brain scans, we would never know. We never did get scanned so, to this day, neither of us knows if we are missing a piece of our corpus callosum or not.

Danylo did not take to breastfeeding—he wouldn't, or couldn't, latch on. That was heartbreaking. For me, those bonding moments between a mother and her baby are priceless. I had the most beautiful nursing experience with

Larissa, so I was sorry I would not get to experience this with Danylo. It saddened me…but it did not come close to how I felt leaving the hospital without him.

Can you imagine leaving the hospital without your baby? My body carried this little being on Earth for nine months and now that he was born, I can't take him home? I mean, how do you go home after giving birth to a bundle of joy, without the bundle? I knew he was in good care, but they were strangers after all. I was devastated and felt so empty having to leave him behind…but I did.

Danylo stayed in the Montreal Children's Hospital for a whole week. I visited every day. Every single day, I went to visit and pumped milk. The nurses gave me a machine to take home to make it easier for me as I kept at it for hours at a time. They really were the most compassionate people in the hospital. Everyone was. We all wanted him to have the best beginning of life, and for me that meant giving him my breast milk. I was not going to give that up. God knows I had plenty.

Thinking back, Danylo staying in hospital for more blood work and monitoring until his platelets were back to a good level, was one of the most difficult times in my life. I hated watching them probe his little foot with needles to take more blood and more blood. *Enough already, leave him alone!*

Yes, I was appreciative of the care they were giving him, but I just wanted him home…where he belonged…where his family were waiting to welcome him.

And so, I pumped and I pumped. Every single day.

And one day, after a week, they finally stopped probing and monitoring and poking him, and Danylo came home. *What a relief!* My baby was home where he belonged.

I monitored his eating. I kept a log of how many ounces he ate. The doctors wanted to make sure he was gaining weight, and he was. We had regular check-ins with his cardiologist and neurologist so they could monitor his progress and issues.

And every time I left, I felt better and better. Danylo was developing well—he was doing just fine, so I continued pumping.

There was one thing, however, that I did notice Danylo did that I never saw Larissa do as a baby. He would literally arch his back like a cat when he showed moments of pain. It seemed to be related to his digestive system. So, after soothing his stomach and giving him colic medicine, I would gently place him on his stomach and he would stop crying. It seemed to work so well for him. Danylo loved being on his stomach, and so I let him be.

I clearly remember the cardiologist's telling me, "The issues are insignificant. There is nothing to be done. Just monitor his progress and continue with regular checkups."

At our last appointment on November 4, 1998, he smiled and said, "I'll see you in six months."

It sounded so reassuring. It was a gentle dismissal of my worst fears.

Danylo passed away seven days later.

What? How can this be real? How, why, am I sitting in a funeral home, making arrangements for my baby boy's funeral? My baby boy. Funerals aren't supposed to be for babies. They are for adults, for our parents. Not him. Not my Danylo.

I had been there before—three years earlier—with my mother, planning my father's funeral. That had been unbearable, yet somehow this was worse. This was unimaginable.

Do they even make caskets for babies?

My mind raced, desperate for anything to hold on to.

It has to be blue for Danylo—and the nicest one they possibly have or can make.

I don't remember many details, just fragments. I know I was there, sitting at the table, nodding along as decisions were being made.

It was a beautiful, sunny day when we arranged his funeral. I remember the light outside. We chose his casket. His father wrote the obituary. Then we had to choose a plot—a permanent resting place for Danylo.

Who buys a burial plot in their thirties? We did—at Notre-Dame-des-

Neiges Cemetery, close to his grandparents on both sides. It was so important for him to be near them.

Even now, twenty-five years later, the memories come in pieces, scattered and incomplete. The visitation stretched from 11:00 a.m. to 10:00 p.m., an endless stream of people coming and going. I remember walking into the funeral parlor, seeing his little body lying there in the casket. His favorite toys surrounded him. He looked so small, so fragile. For a moment, I didn't even recognize him.

The room was filled with flowers, the scent overwhelming. They were everywhere—bright, beautiful, and suffocating all at once. I couldn't believe my eyes. I dropped to the floor, consumed by a wave of grief so heavy I couldn't stand. The rest of the day remains a blur.

The next morning, Danylo's funeral was held in our parish church. It was packed; every pew filled. My Danylo, my sweet boy, was carried in and placed before the altar. As we walked with him to the front, I leaned against the casket, my body trembling with grief, my cries echoing through the solemn space. My poor baby. My heart shattered with every step. Above him, the images of God and baby Jesus welcomed him with open arms.

All of a sudden, the softest sound broke through the silence—tip-tap, tip-tap—tiny footsteps echoing through the vast church. I turned and saw Larissa, our little girl, her small hand wrapped in my sister's who had brought her in.

My sister Lida had taken care of everything—of Larissa, of me, of all the things I couldn't bear to face. She had been the first person I called after 911, and from that moment on, she never left my side. She was grieving too, but somehow, she carried us all, her quiet strength holding me together when I felt like I was unraveling. Even now, that strength remains, an unshakable force for me and my family.

The drive to the cemetery felt like a haze, the heat of the sun clouding my thoughts. As we gathered around the burial site, the hardest and final moment arrived—the lowering of Danylo's casket into the earth. I couldn't bear it. The weight of finality crushed me, a heaviness so profound it stole my breath. The thought of him being cold, of never again wrapping him in warmth, shattered me. How could this be happening? How could I never hold him again? The reality of it was too cruel, too unbearable. Danylo was gone.

As his body was laid to rest, I clung fiercely to one truth: His soul had not left me.

His little body—his 'Earth suit,' as I've come to call it—was gone, but his spirit? That could never die. He would live on in my heart, in my breath, in every whispered prayer. Forever and always.

A week later, the funeral home delivered a package—a collection of sympathy cards, the book of signatures from the visitation, and photographs. Among them were images I hadn't expected—pictures of Danylo in his casket, surrounded by flowers. A memory to keep, a bittersweet gift.

For a long time, I could not bring myself to look at those photos. But eventually, I did. I created a memory box for him, filled with some of his favorite things. At first, I visited that box often, searching for comfort in the items that had once brought him joy. I even kept a piece of his umbilical cord. I wonder why I did that?

Now, I open the box less often. But it's always there—a quiet reminder of his life, his love, and the way he will always be a part of me.

Grief is like that, I've learned. At first it consumes you completely but, over time, it shifts. It never truly leaves, but it finds a quieter place to settle, allowing you to carry on, even as it remains with you. The saying goes "time heals all wounds" but I believe it's not just time that heals, it is what you do with that time that makes all the difference

Shortly after Danylo's passing, the Local Community Service Centre (CLSC) reached out to us, offering therapy to help us through our grief. I agreed, unsure of what else to do.

In those sessions, I poured my heart out to the counsellor. I cried so much that I barely left room for words. She was a stranger, but somehow that made it easier. With her, I felt safe. My husband, on the other hand, was unable to share his pain, to speak about our son's death. He did the exact opposite. Although she wasn't a specialist on grief, I continued to see her. My husband did not and, after a while, I too eventually stopped.

Perhaps it was too soon for us. It was obvious that my husband and I were not grieving the same. How could we? We aren't the same at all. We each cope differently with stresses. Our coping styles for the loss of our son differed so much that it would inevitably cause a lot of stress in our relationship and our family.

Much of those first few weeks is a fog. It's like I went through the motions of getting up, getting our daughter ready for school, and finding things to do besides cry all day until Larissa would be back home from school. Luckily, I was then busy with her until bedtime.

Larissa kept me going. She gave me a routine. She was my rock, my reason to continue. At the tender age of five she was so astute. She would come home from school and check under my glasses to see if I had any fresh tears. I tried hard to do most of my crying when she was at school. She gave me hope and so much comfort when she would tell me about her dreams that Danylo sang to her at night or that she saw him on her pillow.

Was it really a dream? Did he come to her at night while we were all asleep? Did my precious angel connect with his older sister? Yes, he did, to let her know that he had arrived safely in heaven.

We made a sudden but conscious decision to sell our house. It was excruciatingly painful to pass by Danylo's room, to see the empty crib and to feel the coldness in the air. We could never avoid that so long as we lived there. The house sold in less than three weeks.

Was it a hasty decision? Perhaps, but it was the right one. We now had something to look forward to. We were scheduled to move into a brand-new home on April 1, 1999, not too far away from where we had been living. It was a new development with new neighbours—new was good. It was exciting to be picking new colours and materials for this new home. I loved the model home so we didn't even need to make any major adjustments. It was perfect.

Christmas crept up on me way too soon. I didn't know how to be, how to act, what to say. Should I smile? Could I be happy, really?

I love everything about Christmas—the decorating, buying gifts, wrapping presents, baking, listening to carols…but how could I do that just six weeks after Danylo's death?

Six weeks!! Yet I did. I had to. How could we not celebrate Christmas for our five-year-old daughter? She needed Christmas and we needed to create it for her—and for us.

Larissa was into Beanie Babies at that time. Her father would buy her one every time he travelled and that created a beautiful collection for her. A couple of weeks before Christmas, her father took her to a Beanie Baby convention in downtown Montreal. She loved it. In fact, they both did. She was so happy and, of course, daddy's little girl came home with a few new ones to add to her beautiful collection.

Shortly after they got home, the telephone rang. Someone from the convention called to inform us that Larissa had won a Beanie Baby in a contest she had entered. Wow! That was something—she was so excited she had won a Beanie Baby!

Just winning the Beanie Baby was exciting enough, but what a sign when she found out she had won the white angel Beanie Baby with shiny wings. Oh, my goodness…this was a sign from her brother. He wanted her to know that he was okay. He was there with us, his presence forever felt through this angel. Larissa kept this very special Beanie Baby angel encased in a plastic container so it would never get dirty. And today, twenty-five years later, a grown independent woman, Larissa's angel Beanie Baby sits on her headboard in her bedroom, free from its case. Forever and always, Danylo is watching over her, over all of us. Heaven gained an angel, and so did we.

Wherever I went, wherever we would be, Danylo was always with me. I felt his presence so much, it was like I had to take a second glance to see if he was actually there. I had never felt that way before. Larissa felt it too. She would tell me that he would sing to her at night. That brought tears to my eyes and joy to my heart. It was then that I knew he would always be with us.

In January, after the holidays, I decided to return to work at the University, but in a different position. I couldn't go back to the same position—there were too many familiar faces…all the people that shown up to pay their respects.

"Yes, I will go work in another department", I thought.

And that is how I ended up in the Faculty of Management. Timing is everything and there was a temporary assignment that would begin right after the New Year. I applied and was offered the position. I needed to work, I needed to keep busy, to learn something new, to be in a new place where I would feel safe, where no one would really know me, or my story. My supervisor fully supported my developmental assignment. In fact, he said, "Tania, wherever you feel comfortable, we are just happy to have you back."

And so, I returned to work at a new location, in a new environment, with new people to me. Yes, it was safe…at least for a while.

You see grief never really goes away. It continues to show up when it wants to, or when it needs to, at different moments or times in your life. It ignites either the sharp heavy pain of his death, or a beautiful memory of his life. And that's when, all of a sudden, intense emotions resurface…until they pass… until the next time.

The first Easter following Danylo's death was rough. Interestingly, my new office was on the tenth floor facing beautiful Mount Royal. A monumental cross sits on the summit of the mountain and, somewhere not far away, our Danylo rests close to both his grandfathers.

It was an earlier start for me that day. I just wanted to get to the office early. I wanted the holiday weekend to be over as soon as possible. I had no control over the calendar, but I had control of how I would move past it, or at least I thought I did.

My supervisor walked into my office greeting me with a smile and simply asked, "How was your Easter weekend, Tania?"

My lips began to tremble, I started shaking, and all of a sudden, I burst into tears.

I couldn't contain myself, the tears just kept flowing. I became hysterical as I recounted how terrible it was. "Diana, we showed up at my mother's house. The entire family was there gathered around the table, ready to say grace and eat. All along I knew who was missing. How could they be so happy? I thought. I couldn't stomach to be around them. They talked, and they laughed and carried on like nothing ever happened. Really? How could they laugh? What was so funny? I hid in my mother's bedroom and didn't want to come out. But I eventually did, not for anyone else but for my Larissa. I wanted to see her happy and enjoying her time with our family and her beloved cousins. Her father discreetly went into the basement and sat there, almost in isolation, the entire time. Thank goodness for Larissa. If it weren't for her, I'm not sure how I could have gone on."

I cried. I carried on. And then I stopped. Diana looked at me and said, "Tania, I have been watching you come to work every single day with a smile and such positive energy, and I keep asking myself, 'How does she do it?'"

She knew. She had heard. She didn't have to be at the funeral to know. Many from the University community had been and they knew.

Yeah, how did I do it? I was not sure where I got the strength from. Was it from my ancestors of women who buried sons and daughters of their own? They had to carry on, and I was one of them. I was chosen by God to give birth to a pure angel who would serve Him in heaven and guide me here on earth. That is how I was able to go on.

But it took a long while for me to get there. The small changes in our lives helped to create new scenes in my vision, new people in my life, new neighbours, new colleagues, new work, new experiences—new was good. But, despite all the new, the past would often crawl back into my vision. And even after all the other losses I would later face in my life, nothing would ever come close to losing my baby boy, Danylo, nothing.

Danylo's life and passing indelibly marked my life.

My calendar tracked the passing of days until eventually May 22 appeared.

Danylo's first birthday. What would he have looked like? Would he still have dark hair? Would the colour of his eyes have changed? Would he be walking, babbling, talking? What would he sound like?

I would never know all these things.

Time passed and work was going well. We settled nicely into our new home. I got acquainted with our new neighbours; there were so many children around, and that was great for Larissa. In June of that year, we decided to take a family trip—an all-inclusive trip to Mexico. Why not? We needed it and, in fact, at that point we had never really taken an extended family vacation of any kind with Larissa.

What a great family bonding time this will be.

Larissa was excited, and so was I. As we were getting settled on the plane, I glanced to my left side and noticed a familiar face. Terry and her family of three were sitting across from us. Terry was the proud owner of Bambino, the local family-owned furniture store where we had purchased beautiful bedroom sets for our children. We both smiled when we recognized each other. Terry immediately gestured with her hands in a cradle position and innocently asked, "Where's the baby?"

Danylo would have been just over a year old. I quickly nodded my head and sat down. I stayed in my seat the entire time.

I didn't want to go there, and for a while I thought I would not need to… until I did.

We landed, and guess what? Of all the hotels and resorts, Terry and her family were staying at the exact same resort as us. It felt like it was meant to be. Our daughters, aged six and five at the time, were destined to become friends—and so were we. Twenty-five years later, I'm grateful that we still are. In fact, Terry is more than just a friend; she holds a seat on my personal board of directors. She's an avid cheerleader, a steadfast supporter, an advocate for my work and for me, and someone who tells me the truth when I need to hear it most. We've always been there for each other when it mattered and, in many ways, we would come to share a commonality in the outcome of our marriages.

The trip to Mexico will forever be one of my most memorable ones. It not only represented one of the most enjoyable times in my life—new friendships were formed, struggles were left behind, and our family bonded—it also allowed the good Lord to create both a miracle and a heartbreak that was to come.

Just as we were getting ready to head back to the beach, the phone rang.

Who would be calling us here?

Much to my surprise, it wasn't the front desk. It was my sister. She called to tell us that my brother Walter had taken a turn for the worse and they didn't know how long he had. *What?* He had ulcers that ruptured, and his liver was failing. *This can't be true. This can't be happening!*

When we returned home, Walter was still in the hospital. It seemed like he was out of the woods, but that turned out to be a deceiving moment instead.

Tragedy once again struck our family when my dearest brother Walter passed away on June 18, 1999, at the age of forty-three. Heaven received another angel. Danylo was now in the company of both his grandfathers and his amazing uncle.

And there we were, seven months later, once again I was struck with emotional pain and grief. The loss of my brother and my son—same funeral parlor, same viewing room. Looking back, that time was like reliving my son's passing. It was like I was there for Danylo all over again, even though it was my brother in the casket.

Grief overpowered me, and it was only later that I truly felt the loss and pain of my brother Walter's passing. I am so sorry, Walter. Not a day goes by that I do not think of you. How much I would have loved for you to meet my sons, to have conversations with you, to just hear your soft voice and your laughter, and to see your charismatic self.

I knew that eventually something good had to happen to us because while bad things happen to good people, good things happen too. And sometimes they happen at the same time. I felt we had endured enough suffering to last us a lifetime.

And good did happen. In fact, a miracle was bestowed upon us and the joy that only a mother could ever really know. I became pregnant…a surprise to many, ourselves included!

On March 25, 2000, we were blessed with another beautiful son, Adrian Christopher. Another boy! We were elated. They say that usually you have the opposite of what you lose but here we were having another son. It was a miracle indeed.

Adrian filled our hearts and home with so much joy. It was like I was given another chance for our million-dollar family. Well, I had more than that. With a daughter and son on Earth, and one beautiful son in heaven, I had everything…and that is how it was supposed to be for me.

Everything went smoothly with the pregnancy until I was about to give birth. During the final stretch of pushing, the doctor suddenly said: "Stop pushing, stay still." And I did…as I waited for him to untangle the umbilical cord from around my baby's neck. I froze, literally and figuratively, until it was safe for the final push. And out he came.

I didn't know how I would be with Adrian as a newborn. Although from the get-go he didn't feel like a newborn. Weighing nine pounds, eight ounces at birth, it was like I already had a two-month-old.

Adrian was a good baby. Much like his sister, he ate and slept really well. Nursing him was so enjoyable, reminding me of the time I nursed Larissa. He latched on easily and I nursed him for over nine months…there is no greater feeling for a mother and her newborn!

I felt relaxed with Adrian. He had a clean bill of health. I was so relieved and reassured. I knew this was different. This would be different. Each experience is. That is one thing I did know for sure. I did not, could not, allow Danylo's death to instill fear in how I would be with Adrian. Perhaps it's because I knew Adrian did not have any health issues of concern and my living with the fact that Danylo's death was an isolated tragedy.

Adrian is the miracle that came after losing Danylo. I cannot imagine life without him and believe wholeheartedly he is meant to be here—for me to have two sons, one on Earth and one in heaven. God gave me these three blessings even though he needed Danylo in heaven to serve Him and the kingdom, but mostly for Danylo to watch over us. I have been blessed with a guardian angel for life.

I never really worried about Adrian when he was a baby…worrying is not in my nature. But still, there were a few moments. One day I was in the middle of washing the dishes when I suddenly stopped what I was doing and quickly ran upstairs to his crib. The monitor was on but I gently placed my finger under his nose to make sure he was breathing. Ah yes! That was all I needed to feel.

Unlike our first house, we now lived in a cottage where all the bedrooms were upstairs. That monitor was always on and so was my habit of checking his breathing. In fact, this remained a practice I did for almost twelve years. No matter where we lived, where we were, it was just a given. Before I could go to sleep, I would quietly walk into Adrian's room and gently place my finger under his nose so I could feel the air coming out. It gave me the peace of mind I needed, even though I didn't really need it.

Having Adrian enriched our lives and, perhaps, filled a void. It is a void that I know can never really be filled, but I accepted my reality and felt blessed and grateful for the miracle of another son. I saw that life could bring us joy despite the tremendous pain and grief we endured losing Danylo.

My husband, however, could not seem to really find joy. I was the only one who really (re)found joy in life.

And so, we continued to function like a family. We had delightful children, a beautiful home, and careers in which we were both successful, and yet it is like we were unable to return to a place of peace within our relationship and our environment.

I realized that, as a couple, we were two very different people who did not grieve in the same way. And we never really respected how opposingly different our grieving processes were from each other. Our personalities were—are—so different. I travelled far and worked hard to get out of the victim mode. A shining light guided me, and I kept moving toward it. It was too hard for me to stay in the pain.

It eventually became clear that our outlooks on life clashed and that we were on opposing sides of our grief spectrums. How then could we support each other in a meaningful way?

A survivor's response to loss is significantly conditioned by their model of the world and their reality and judgement about how the world works. Talking and sharing the story of a loss can bring emotional relief for survivors, promote their search for meaning, and bring people together in mutual support. This is what it did for me…when I finally felt I could open up and share my grief.

And, bit by bit, year after year, I did. It was a journey that I deliberately paced and protected, because talking and sharing was not something I could comfortably do at home. Danylo's name was hardly ever mentioned, except with my children.

That surprised me but, in an ironic way, it prepared me for what would eventually lead me to embrace my pain with deeper purpose. The compartmentalization of that pain was all part of the plan. One thing I knew for sure, I would never stop saying Danylo's name and today, more than ever, his name is being heard. There is a warm tingle inside of me whenever I say his name, a radiant smile when I realize what his short life on Earth meant for me. Twenty-five years later, I am honoring Danylo's life and legacy in the most beautiful and profound way that I can—by sharing him with the world.

BRINGING LIGHT TO LOSS

The wound is the place where the light enters you.

Rumi

Pain has a way of demanding attention. It grips us, forcing us to slow down and confront what we often avoid. But, within the heaviness of pain, lies the invitation to see the light—to create meaning and purpose from it, to grow through it.

Bringing Light to Loss aims to illuminate the transformative power of loss, focusing on the acceptance that where there is love, there will be loss. Where there is loss, there will be pain. But pain is not meant to be a destination; it is a passage, asking us to keep moving, not to stay stuck. And, like all passages, it carries us toward hope—revealing that even in the darkest moments, we are not meant to live in the hurt, but to rise from it.

Drawing upon Elizabeth Kubler-Ross' renowned work on the five stages of grief—shock and denial, anger, bargaining, depression, and acceptance—my memoir shows how I healed through this process. It details and delves into how my acceptance of Danylo's death has, over the years, transformed into something so meaningful—my internal peace and freedom.

It is in acceptance that we find the strength to heal, to embrace loss with hope and gratitude, and to move forward while carrying the beautiful memories of what was lost. Because "Death is not the greatest loss in life. The greatest loss is what dies inside us while we live."

— *Norman Cousins*

I refused to die inside, and I know that Danylo would never have let that happen. He is my strength, he is my courage, he is my reason to continue.

This is my story, but if you too are a sufferer of loss, I hope I can inspire you reach a place where you can accept and embrace loss and not let yourself die within. Our life's journeys include both good and bad moments which are so often intertwined. It is essential to believe, to have faith, and to understand that we have a higher purpose beyond ourselves. By continuing to live and bring hope to others, we can fulfill that purpose, even in the face of the most devastating losses.

Grief is a lifelong journey. Irrespective of the phases or stages, it never ends…and that's okay. Over time, it becomes lighter, less overwhelming, and we eventually find peace in the loss. Happiness begins to reappear, not because the grief disappears, but because you grow stronger with each passing day.

After all these years, I realized that the way out of my pain is through serving and helping others. At the same time, it allows me to continuously remember and honor what was lost. It seems like this was already part of God's plan. This is my calling. While pain and grief never truly disappear, they transform in the way you choose to approach them. The question is: How will you choose to approach your pain?

In *My Grandmother's Hands*, Resmaa Menakem explains that there are two kinds of pain. There is clean pain and there is dirty pain. I was intrigued by this and inspired by how it brought clarity to how I managed my own pain. Clean pain, though it hurts deeply, allows our bodies to grow through difficulties, to develop resilience, and heal trauma. It's the sadness, hurt, or sorrow that comes from the situation itself, and it helps you heal over time.

It is part of the grieving process and, over time, it creates space for growth, freeing up energy that was once protected. This type of pain helps us build capacity for transformation. It is what we experience when we know what needs to be done and, even though we resist it, we ultimately act from the best parts of ourselves. As a wife and mother, I did what I needed to do and I carried on with life—despite my loss *and* because of it. Because my angel was guiding me.

Dirty pain, on the other hand, stems from avoidance, blame, or denial. It is the pain of running away, physically or emotionally, and it often deepens our hurt and the hurt of others. It comes from the stories and negative thoughts we add on top of the pain. It is the guilt, anger, shame, or blaming ourselves or others that often comes with grief.

Yes, we do go through all these stages in the grieving process, but I now see the difference. Dirty pain keeps us stuck and does not help the healing. It is like extra emotional baggage we carry, preventing us from moving forward. It is the pain from previous traumas that we carry unhealed in our bodies and which eventually show up in heavier, cloudier, and unhealthier ways. Because the pain was never healed, our bodies automatically freeze and we let our minds convince us to stay and add more layers to our grief.

When profound grief strikes, like the loss of a child, dirty pain is inevitable. And, in varying degrees, it can stay with us for a long time.

Why does it stay more for some and less for others? In one way it is a choice and, in another way, it is an inherent trait that has been passed down through generational trauma—trauma that was never healed and continues to permeate within the body. Healing really comes when we are able to transition from dirty pain to clean pain, freeing ourselves to find purpose and meaning once again. No two people process pain the same way, and every single person will journey through the process of pain based on who they are.

I realized that a way out of my pain was to continue to live with purpose—for myself and for my family—and, eventually, to enlighten others. Although I have always felt that sharing and teaching was an inherent characteristic of mine, I never thought I would use my life's losses to help heal others, or that my son Danylo would be the catalyst for this work. Choosing this path speaks to my view of life: To live with an outward focus, even amidst any of my own struggles.

This is the journey I chose—the one I embrace as I share my stories of loss while aspiring to help others heal, triumph over pain, and live with the same love and purpose I do…because, deep down, I know it's possible.

For as long as I can remember, writing has been my sanctuary. It is where I allow my emotions to flow freely, like a river carving its way through the landscape of my soul. In quiet moments, pen in hand, I find release, comfort, and clarity. Books and books fill with my writings—thoughts, brain dumped and journaled—are all neatly tucked away in my office. Those pages, filled with my innermost thoughts, are my refuge. I love what writing brings to me: the flow of extraction, the slow untangling of chaos, and the creation of peace within my thoughts and soul.

That's how the journey to writing this book began. It was a tremendous download—days and nights of uninterrupted writing poured from me like a stream that had been waiting for its moment of release. Now the task is to piece it all together and to weave structure and meaning into the words as I continue to uncover the purpose behind it all.

This is the birth of *Bringing Light to Loss*, a story not just about my journey, but also about the journey of the spirited women in my family. Interwoven with generations of loss, pain, struggle and, ultimately, hope, gratitude, and love, this is our collective legacy—a legacy of resilience that transcends time and place, showing us what it truly means to be free from suffering.

Resilience, I've learned, is not just an action but a way of being. It is a quiet strength that courses through our veins, shaped by the hands and hearts of those who came before us. As Resmaa Menakem beautifully expresses in *My Grandmother's Hands*, "resilience is absorbed and expressed in our relationships with family, community, and the world". The thick skin I carry was forged long before my time, passed down by my ancestors. I am honored to hold it, and grateful for the strength it brings me each and every day.

I was meant to experience profound pain, because God knew I could handle it. I was meant to give birth to an angel and to carry his spirit with me, letting him guide me and remind me every day of the message I am here to share through my hands, my heart, and my soul.

Now, I invite you to pause for a moment. What pain are you holding onto right now? Can you feel its weight, its presence in your body and mind?

What if, instead of holding on, you chose a different path—a luminous path that creates space for your own growth and the growth of others? What might that look like for you?

LIFE AFTER DANYLO

Grief is the price we pay for love.
Queen Elizabeth II

I often felt Danylo's presence. He was with us daily. Especially in the playroom of our new home. This was the space where Adrian and Larissa played—sometimes together, sometimes apart. Despite the six-and-a-half-year age gap, Larissa always made time for her little brother, and he adored his big sister. Every day when she came home from school, she would run to greet Adrian, no matter where he was.

The playroom was spacious, complete with a separate glassed-in toy room, full of playful wonder and plenty of room for their imaginations to roam. I would sit on the couch or the floor, and I felt Danylo there too. I often found myself doing a double take—because he was there…I swear I felt him playing with us.

When Adrian was little, he'd point to Danylo's picture, smile brightly, and say, "Baby." I'd always respond with a soft smile and say, "That's Danylo."

As he grew older, it amazed me how naturally he spoke of his brother, as if they had met and had shared memories together.

I still remember the day Adrian started pre-kindergarten. One afternoon, the children were asked to draw a picture of their family. At just four years old, their portraits were charmingly simple stick figures with big smiles and lopsided heads. Adrian proudly showed me his drawing. Right there in the center, among the crayon-sketched figures of me, his father, and his big sister Larissa, was Danylo.

My heart swelled with warmth and, at the same time, an ache of uncertainty. How would he answer if someone asked about his brother? Would he say, "He's in heaven"? Would he call him an angel?

Danylo *was* our angel—and at moments like this, I was reminded again just how deeply his presence lived on in us.

It was a beautiful summer day in June 2004. The sun was shining brightly and the sky was a perfect blue. I was driving downtown to interview for my dream job—the position of Human Resources Advisor in the Faculty of Engineering, a significant step up in my career. I remember wearing a lovely baby-blue designer suit my sister had gifted me—a gift that wasn't just clothing, but a reflection of her generosity and how deeply she cares for me. Whether it's an impromptu postcard in the mail, a cup with our picture on it, or a thoughtful note just when I need it most, she always finds unique ways to demonstrate her love for me. Her thoughtfulness seems to show up exactly when I need it and I am truly lucky to have her.

Suddenly *My Immortal* by Evanescence began to play on the radio and, just like that, tears suddenly streamed down my face. Those words, that melody, just shook me. All I could think of was Danylo. He was my immortal. I looked out the window at that beautiful blue sky and I saw his silhouette watching over me. What a feeling! He was riding along in the car with me and, amidst the tears, a smile broke through.

When I parked, I took a moment to regroup before making my way to the building. I entered the familiar elevator and rode it to the fifteenth floor, poised and ready to meet the committee. They were all present as I confidently entered the interview room. The questions began and continued, one after another, for the next hour. Finally, it was over. I sighed in relief. I had done it!

The following week, I received a call telling me the job was mine. Working in the Faculty of Engineering not only elevated my career but also connected me with incredible people. One special person I met was Enza, who had started just two weeks before me. *Could this be the work of my angel?*

Enza and I hit it off immediately. Our energy was electric, and we had so much fun in the office. She quickly became not just a colleague, but also one of my dearest friends. Fast forward to today, and Enza has become an integral part of my life—someone who shares in my adventures, sorrows, and triumphs. She is a true gem, a great soul, and holds a high place on my personal board of directors. Early in our friendship, I remember her saying, "Tania, you have a story to tell, and one day you will write a book."

Thank you, Enza, for planting that seed and for being in my life. You were right—I do have a story, and so do you! One day I hope you too will write your own story!

I cannot tell you how many times Danylo appeared when we most needed him. Larissa's high school graduation was a particularly exciting time, especially as we shopped for her prom dress. We found the most beautiful classic navy-blue gown—simple, ageless, and elegant. It fitted her like a glove and with the pearl necklace and earrings I wore on my wedding day, she channeled Audrey Hepburn and looked absolutely stunning!

But that day almost didn't happen. As we drove home from dress shopping, the gown safely on the back seat, a massive eighteen-wheeler truck came out of nowhere and collided with us nearly pushing us into the highway barrier. Miraculously, while the left side of the car sustained significant damage, we were spared. I sat in shock, unable to comprehend what had just occurred. I glanced at Larissa who was equally stunned and began to cry. Frazzled by the accident, I remained glued to my seat, unsure of what to do. I looked up to the sky, and there was Danylo's silhouette, reassuring me that Larissa and I would be okay. He was watching over us, protecting us from what could have been a fatal accident. The car was totaled, but we were alive. We still had more life to live, love to share, and service to give. It was not our time.

On prom night, Larissa glowed in her dress as she took to the floor for the memorable father-daughter dance.

I never fully understood the depth of Larissa's pain or how Danylo's death affected her. I believed that, like me, she was simply carrying on with life, compartmentalizing her emotions even though she was in so much pain. Not many little five-year-old girls go to school one day sharing the cute things their baby brother does, only to lose him the next day. I wonder if she ever told anyone about her grief. Maybe she was like me when I was fifteen and in denial about my parents' separation—I did not share my feelings about that until almost a year later.

I only began to realize the pain Larissa felt when I came across one of her grade ten high school papers. She was fifteen years old at the time. Her paper happened to be saved on my computer and, by chance, I saw it. The assignment was to write a short descriptive paper about a memorable childhood recollection. I imagine most students wrote about their first ballet recital, their first trip to Granby Zoo, or Disneyland, but my daughter poignantly wrote every single detail about the day her brother died. As I read each, line by line, my eyes watered and tears poured uncontrollably down my face. My heart broke for her, for me, for all of us. Little did I know her pain. How would I? How could I? We never really talked about it…until years later.

What struck me most was *what* she wrote. What was in her little mind when tragedy struck our family?

Our house was full of people—so many faces, some familiar, but many not. Larissa was in the basement with the police officers. She sat at her desk with all her art supplies, a colouring book, and her favorite pink baby doll right beside her. She was determined to show the police officer how well she could colour and keep within the lines. She removed a page from her colouring book—a picture of a duck—and spent a great amount of time colouring the entire picture without going over the lines. She wanted it to be perfect.

The officer was so impressed with her colouring. Larissa shyly presented him with her picture and then, with natural curiosity, she inched her way up the stairs probably wondering 'Where is my mommy?'.

Amidst the crowd and chaos, something I am sure she never experienced before in her life and hopefully never will again, she found me on the couch, motionless, rocking her lifeless baby brother, all wrapped up in his blanket.

I needed to keep him warm because that is what a mother is supposed to do. Isn't it?

Part of life is learning to accept what is. But how do we make peace with the terrible things that happen to us? Can we ever truly accept them?

Sometimes, in our pain, we look for someone to blame. At first, I was angry, blaming God and myself for my son's death. Then, after a while, I understood the anger behind it and, while it hurt, I didn't let it add to the overwhelming grief I already carried. I knew I had not harmed my baby... and neither had God.

I wasn't there when Danylo passed into heaven, but I often wondered: Could I have prevented it?

For a long time, I carried the weight of guilt—the guilt of not being able to protect my baby. Even now, I find myself revisiting that night, replaying every detail in my mind, wondering what more I could have done. And then I remind myself to let it go. I know nothing can change what happened. The past is the past. Parents are supposed to protect their children, that's how it is supposed to be, but I've also learned that sometimes life unfolds beyond our control. It was how it was meant to be, even if it didn't, and still doesn't, make sense to me.

Every year, on the eve of Danylo's passing, I wake up at 5:30 a.m.—the same time I woke on November 11, 1998. It is like clockwork. I open my eyes, I scan the room, and I know he's there, right beside me. Danylo, in his beautiful christening gown, gifted by his godmother Lesia, framed with the words:

An angel found of purest love
is sent to you from God above.
Ever watchful and always true,
an angel meant for only you.

Yes, my angel.

Resilience isn't born overnight. It's crafted, piece by piece, from the challenges we face—and the shields we build to survive them. Looking back, I realize I've been building my shield ever since my earliest memories, every layer shaped by the hardships of my childhood. It became my way of protecting myself—a shield that allowed me to move at my own pace and to internally process things until I was ready to face them in the real world.

Much like the glass that shields Larissa's Beanie Baby angel, my coping mechanism kept me safe and intact. By compartmentalizing my emotions, I controlled how I showed up—for myself, and for others. It felt safe. It worked.

But here's the thing: life doesn't wait for you to be ready. Loss, death, trauma—they happen on *their* terms, not ours. I thought I was in control but life, with its unexpected turns, made sure to remind me that I wasn't. It has surprised me, and forced me into moments where I had no choice but to confront my emotions and grief head-on.

And you know what? That was part of the plan all along. It's messy and it hurts but that's how healing works.

Looking back, I wonder: Was there something, someone, guiding me through it all? Was I doing it alone? Or was I guarded by an angel who kept me calm through the storms? Did I create her in my mind? Was she a gift from God? Maybe it was my grandmother, Tetiana, the one I never had the chance to meet. Or perhaps it was simply my own ability to summon those angels, those guardian figures that guided and protected me until I could face things on my own terms.

In the end, it doesn't matter who or what they were. They helped me heal. This is how I chose to heal—to believe in them, and they in me. Because I let them in.

PATTERNS OF THE PAST

Until you make the unconscious conscious,
it will direct your life, and you will call it fate.
Carl Jung

Ultimately, we all have the ability to make choices in our lives, and we are the ones responsible for our own actions.

Charles R. Swindoll claims that "life is ten percent what happens to you and ninety percent how you react to it." He elaborates on the concept, emphasizing the significance of attitude in shaping experiences. This is where we have a choice to decide—to either stay in the challenge, in the sorrow, in the struggle, or to face it head on and say: Yes, this happened to me, this is what I am living now, I got it. I accept it. I hate it, but now what?

What could I do to get past my tragedy and move on?

I showed myself that I *could*. It took a lot of courage to adapt to Danylo's death, but I had to. I had a reason to continue. I had a family I loved; a beautiful daughter who brought joy into my life each and every day. I had a life to live, and I did. I was guided by my angels, and I believe wholeheartedly that they showed me the light, that there was hope, and, most importantly, that I had a life to live…and I wanted to continue to live it to the fullest.

I saw the light. In fact, it is always there…it just took me a little longer to see it.

Confrontation was not something that I dealt with well. In fact, more often than not, I would avoid it if I could. But that is not real life, is it? I may have not welcomed it…it just showed up! And it has shown up many times in my life, including in my marriage.

Our disagreements weren't so much about opinions or thoughts—that I could have appreciated. In fact, I found those conversations very stimulating and even enlightening. My husband was well read, keen-minded, and knowledgeable about many subjects and I valued his intelligence. I was fascinated by how much he knew about literally everything. His friends use to call him a walking encyclopedia and I felt the same way. He was an exceptional writer and the love letters and beautiful cards he wrote to me were treasures in their own right. Not to mention that while he travelled across the continent for work, he would send Larissa and I weekly cards. They were priceless. In his own way, he was such a kind and loving man, hence my initial attraction to him, our eight-year courtship of love, and our twenty-year marriage.

On the other hand, walking on eggshells is not something I was comfortable with. Not knowing if an altercation was brewing—not because milk was spilled on the table, a ball was accidently thrown onto the glass wall, or the gate was left open and the dog ran away—but because of who he was, what he was suffering inside, his nature, his character, and the state of mind he was in during these moments.

So, what were his triggers? Honestly, I never fully understood. Because it was foreign to me, I did not understand, and I did not remain curious enough to want to. I just knew it didn't feel right, and I didn't know how to navigate it. The children and I became recipients of his outbursts, and maybe I even contributed to them. They say it takes two to tango, but neither of us seemed to know how to do that well.

The dating and fantasy romance of love eventually transcended into a relationship of challenges and struggles. I became more compassionate and more interested in mental health. There was an awareness brewing around mental health making it easier to talk about and accept but, at the time, I never really knew how to deal with it effectively…or deal with it at all.

The thing is, the patterns were there and would remain…patterns that seemed a little too familiar to me. Perhaps not exactly the same because, of course, no two people are alike and nothing is ever the same. I had been a child then, so what did I know except to cocoon myself away from the behavior…but now I was the adult, the partner, the wife, and the recipient of those behaviors, whether intentional or not.

But cocooning and avoidance only lasts so long. As much as I did not want to face it, eventually I had to. As time passed, I began to see differences in my own behavior. I became more vocal, less tolerant, and I would react. I would say things like, "Are you crazy? You are getting mad because of that?"

Not exactly the response anyone wants to hear, right?

I remember coming home from an Easter brunch with my family and mother-in-law after an uncomfortable conversation at the restaurant. Interestingly, I cannot even recall what it was about but, once at home, I became confrontational and started to raise my voice. That was something I would not normally do, especially in front of children or family…but this time it felt different.

My mother-in-law—God rest her beautiful soul, she was the kindest and most loving mother-in-law and grandmother and we were so fortunate to have her in our lives—asked me to stay quiet, not to say anything, not to poke the bear and make things worse. That's when I turned to her and said, "This is not acceptable."

And I blurted out, "Why should I keep quiet? Where is this anger coming from?"

To what extent do I have to tolerate this behavior, to accept it as okay? Is it okay? Love can only take you so far. Oh, I can take, oh yes, I can love and I can take, and I can take…until I can't take it anymore.

My mother-in-law looked at me and said, "You know, Tania, I feel I am to blame."

"Why would you say that? You are not are not responsible for anyone else's behavior or actions."

She explained, "You see, Tania, I had my firstborn very young, just nineteen years old, and almost every week I would call my pediatrician. You know, he was like a family doctor to me, a father figure of sorts. I was anxious and needed reassurance. I would ask him questions to reassure me about anything that came up with the baby. So, when I was feeling insecure, unsure of what I was doing, I would dial Dr. R. One day, while on a call with him, he said to me, 'Missus, there is nothing wrong with your son, but there is something seriously wrong with you. I think you should get help.'"

Wow, my eyes widened hearing that! What a moment—what a revelation!

"Tania," she continues, "I didn't get the help I needed, and I regret that now."

But who would have thought of getting that kind of help in those days? Seriously, it just wasn't something you did.

In that moment, I just carried on with the conversation but I often wondered what it must have been like for her as a mother at just nineteen years of age. Of course, who wouldn't have questions, doubts, or fears? She was practically a child herself. She had just wanted assurance and held on to the doctor's insights as much as possible. He gave her reassurance, and that's what she needed.

Maybe she felt like there was no-one else she could approach…or maybe she felt too ashamed to ask. He was her doctor and, perhaps, she felt most comfortable speaking with him about her concerns. I never quite asked her so I will never really know, but I have come to realize that she did the best that she could and, for that, I commend her.

I will never forget that living-room conversation because it was somewhat of a watershed moment. It made me appreciate her even more than I had and, at the same time, it provided an insight into her coping skills as she navigated motherhood while also shedding light on the effects it had on both her and her children.

It became clear to me that this anxious behaviour had permeated through her lifetime and it most likely was passed down through generations before her. While raising her children, she unknowingly passed on the same behaviours which she witnessed, and tried to shield me from, in her adult offspring.

There is no blame or shame here, just a better understanding of how behavioral patterns are prevalent in all of our lives. You see, children do not learn by what we tell them to do (or not to do), but rather by what they are exposed to on a regular basis every day of their lives. Most mothers, including my mother-in-law, do not understand the repercussions of their actions, behaviors, and words on their children until they see it in them.

The behaviors, attitudes, and reactions that children are exposed to in their home lives shape who they become. While personality and character play a role, much of what we carry forward is conditioned by our early environment. I remember my mother-in-law once taking a popsicle out of the freezer and running it under water before giving it to her granddaughter, Larissa. In that small, seemingly insignificant moment, she was passing on a behavior that may still echo through our family today.

So, while my mother-in-law may not have fully understood how behavioral patterns take root, her presence often felt marked by innocence and curiosity—much like my own. It was her son, however, who carried a certain weight of anger, and that's what we were often exposed to. I had seen some glimpse of his outbursts toward her even before we were married, but I turned a blind eye. Perhaps she had done the same. Or perhaps, in her own quiet way, she had simply grown used to the storm.

And in many ways, I welcomed her curiosity throughout our married life. She was always so interested and genuinely curious about everything—especially the children. She loved hearing their stories and took great pride in all their accomplishments, both academic and recreational. She was a big fan and would come to as many events and shows as possible—Ukrainian dancing, swimming, and synchronized swimming competitions… whether real or pretend.

I say "pretend" because we had a swimming pool at home, and every summer she would come by to watch how the children progressed and immersed themselves in their love of the sport. Playing judge and scoring their performances was such a treat—not just for them, but for her as well.

That adoration survived our marital problems. Certainly, there was tension when things were unravelling, but she remained actively involved in our lives. I remember one day, years later, she asked me, "Tania, can I still call you, my daughter-in-law?" and I happily responded, "Yes, I will always be your daughter-in-law."

We maintained a close relationship, something she did not expect. Love conquered all, and there was simply no reason to not continue to show respect for one another. She was not responsible for how my relationship with my husband unfolded…that was between us. As she aged, the children and I continued to visit and speak with her on a regular basis and I am truly grateful that my son, Adrian, and I were there for her on her last day on Earth before she too joined Danylo and the family in heaven.

She was a wonderful compassionate, devoted, and caring woman. She will always be a mother-in-law to me.

For the longest time, I questioned whether our communication styles— or lack thereof—exacerbated the issues between my husband and I. Looking back, I realize we rarely had heart-to-heart conversations about our needs or desires. Come to think of it, neither did my parents.

When we were first married, my husband travelled for work outside of Montreal during the week and we would only see each other on weekends. I remember people would say, "Tania, you have the best of both worlds—you have your freedom and the security of marriage." This arrangement went on for several years and allowed me to simply be me. Maybe, too much so.

I *did* feel an incredible sense of freedom. It was as if I were forever in the honeymoon stage of life. I continued to nurture close relationships with my friends, which brought me so much joy—especially with my dearest friend, Anna, who holds one of the most special places in my heart

After I had Larissa, Anna would often cycle over to my place. Those visits were a balm for both of us, offering peace and a sense of freedom amid life's ongoing challenges. Larissa absolutely adored Anna, and the bond we formed during those years has endured for nearly forty years.

Anna may feel blessed to have me in her life, but the truth is, I feel the greatest blessing. She has been a living example of the kind of family I always wanted to embrace—one rooted in love, support, and togetherness. While our families may not share the same traditional structure, we share the same deep values and commitment to nurturing those we love. And ultimately, that is what matters most.

My weeks were filled with what I loved—supporting my friends, spending time with my family, diving into my personal interests like dancing and engaging in the community, and, of course, school.

I did have the best of both worlds. But was that really how it was supposed to be?

In many ways, our marriage served its purpose, while allowing us to overlook the signs and downplay the lack of what we needed most—meaningful communication. I wish I had known then what I know now about the importance of communication. By the time my husband's work environment changed and he started working from home more frequently, I had already begun to withdraw. I shared less and made less effort. It felt easier to ignore or block things out rather than confront them…until my frustrations would boil over, leading me to react without thinking. Unsurprisingly, that didn't help the situation.

In time, I began to see the effects our strained relationship was having on our children. It started to resemble my childhood. That was when I knew something had to change. I hoped things would improve and eventually they did—because I made it happen.

The peace and harmony I strive for—whether at home, work, or anywhere else—has become my unwavering mission. Living in an environment that feels safe and nurturing is all I've ever wanted. I yearn for a place that allows me to feel my best and frees my spirit to be whole. It doesn't need to be grand or filled with material things, it simply needs to radiate joy, belonging, happiness, and love. Plain and simple.

Today, that is exactly what I've created in my home. I am surrounded by the things and memories that bring me happiness—my children's photos, their achievements and milestones, colourful images I hold in my mind and in reality, pictures of my family, my love, reminders of my accomplishments, and books…lots and lots of books. But most importantly, my home is filled with peace and quiet. Chaos and toxicity are left at the door, for there is no place or room for them in my life anymore.

Family is important, and from a young age I learned that no matter how much we might disagree with our siblings, parents, or relatives, they can never be replaced. A husband, boyfriend, or friend can. I am still not sure if those were the wisest words for me to hear, but maybe they were. Certainly, blood is thicker than water but doesn't there come a time when the bond between a couple takes precedence over family?

I'm not sure if I ever fully received that message, or maybe I did but chose to ignore it. When I faced struggles within my relationship, it was all too easy to side with my family. Perhaps I wanted to be seen as a loving couple, for "us" to be accepted by them, too much. I realize now that I didn't need their acceptance; I needed to accept myself and see my reality for what it was.

I did actually come to that realization, but often I looked the other way or made excuses for certain behaviors. I longed for the fairy-tale ending, the perfect family but, as it turned out, that dream would be shattered, and the real "happily ever after" would come much later.

As much as I didn't want to hear my family's comments, they were true… but I needed to discover that for myself. And this in no way takes away from the goodness and tremendous big heart that my husband showed me over the years, and still does today. That is real. But so were the struggles.

THE HEALING JOURNEY

Healing is not about fixing what's broken.
It's about nurturing what's still alive.
Tasha Eurich

I needed to be in that *Helping Relationships* course, it was part of my master's program in Education, Human Relations and Family Life which I started in the fall of 2002.

In fact, I needed to be in that specific program because countless revelations awaited me.

Initially, I had considered pursuing a Master of Education with a focus on curriculum design, but something led me to this path instead. It is fascinating how my intuition guided me there, and always directed me to the places where I needed to learn and grow. I was exactly where I was meant to be.

That degree prompted me to dig deep into my personal life and become aware of things I had previously overlooked. It opened doors to a wealth of truths, emotions, and deeper self-reflection, creating space for healing and preparing me to embrace what lay ahead. It marked a major transformation in my life.

If I think about it, it was in June of 2008 when I was officially awarded my Master of Education, Human Relations and Family Life degree. That same summer would mark another new and difficult chapter of my life.

During one of our classes, we were asked to write a research paper on a topic of interest. I was eager to dive into work/life balance—a very relevant topic for me in the early 2000s as I was juggling raising a young family, building a career in higher education, and pursuing my master's part-time. I embarked on the journey with dedication and, just as I had embraced my undergraduate degree which took me nine years to complete, I approached this program with the same level of commitment.

Each course, each semester, was a step up the hill on Peel Street to the Faculty of Education. Naturally, this faculty was situated atop a hill, just below the Mount Royal—a mountain that would become more significant for me in later years. Despite the harsh winters and the lonely walks to my car at night, I was not discouraged. I kept going, I kept walking, I kept learning, and I kept growing.

Working at McGill University, the same institution where I pursued my degree, was a significant advantage. No matter how bad the weather was, I rarely missed a class. I moved through the program at my own pace, with no external pressure, just an internal drive and motivation to see it through. I was determined to achieve more than just an undergraduate degree. I wanted my master's degree to deepen my learning and apply it across all areas of my life. True learning and growth come from applying the knowledge we gain and embracing the insights that arise when we open ourselves to understanding. As Aristotle wisely said, "Knowing thyself is the beginning of all wisdom." And that, indeed, is no easy feat.

With a husband travelling for work most of the time, I often found myself carrying a lot of the weight when it came to the children and family. However, in many ways, I enjoyed it. It made it easier to manage and make decisions on the spot. I loved it—the freedom to choose, to make decisions on my own because I had to, and because I wanted to. Maybe I loved it too much.

The topic of career/life balance really resonated with me. I was drawn to learn more about it, seeking knowledge and perspectives from experts and others on how to harmonize these aspects of life, because it was something I could relate to. I wanted to be the best mother and wife I could be while managing my career and personal interests. Can you relate?

Life often requires sacrifices. There were times when I couldn't attend my child's field trip, be present at school functions, or host as many playdates as other mothers could. Some things didn't receive the attention they deserved, but I did my best to make it work. I believe I was there for what truly mattered—the morning hellos, mealtimes, bedtime snuggles, storytelling, and witnessing the creation of their unique stories every day as they grew older and added new chapters to their lives.

As women I feel we wear multiple hats and play many different roles. I still remember my mother's words, "Tania, in life you will play many roles—daughter, wife, lover, mother, psychologist, coach, homemaker, lawyer, banker, social planner, family counsellor…among others that inherently show up when skill and work is needed."

Wow, that's quite the repertoire of skills and responsibilities we have! Who ever came up with that?

I call her Wonder Woman. Funny, when I think of *Wonder Woman*, the show I loved watching back in the 1980s, I can't help but think of Amy Cuddy who, in her book *Presence* refers to Wonder Woman when striking a "power pose." The Wonder Woman or superhero stands tall with her feet shoulders-width apart, places her hands on her hips, and lifts her chin slightly.

Imagine yourself as a superhero, ready to conquer any challenge that comes your way. I love this pose, and it is one that I do on a regular basis. Adding affirmations while looking in the mirror for approximately two minutes is even better. When my confidence levels are low—before an interview or when having difficult conversations with supervisors or loved ones—this pose helps me reframe my thoughts and gives me the energy I need to feel empowered.

It has been said that power posing has a reliable effect on our thoughts, feelings, mood, self-esteem, feelings of dominance…among others. And that is why I do it!

I came to realize that career and work aren't things you really balance. Sure, we can create a timeframe for a regular workday as nine to five, and assume that life after work is five to nine…but is it really?

Today, everything seems blurred and so much more interconnected. Our lives in general have become more integrated. Now it seems to be less about the distinct roles that each person plays, and more about how that person *shows up* in any role—wife, mother, daughter, student, employee, coach, teacher, friend…wholeheartedly, genuinely, themselves.

Recently, I heard a quote from Dan Ponterfract: "*Our lives shape our work, our work shapes us*".

This could not be truer. We need to understand how we feel in both areas of our life, to see how they influence each other…because they do. Personal and marital problems will affect everything you do, even your work. It is hard to keep strong emotions in check all the time and, as much as we don't want to bring personal issues into our workspace, inevitably they will show up. The question is, how do they show up? And how do you handle them?

Although I was initially drawn to the topic of career and work/life balance, which would later become the foundation of my program 'Be the CEO of Your Career and Life' and my passion for personal development, I found myself taking a different direction. At the library, I researched books and authors on the subject of career and family, however, a deeper and more compelling force was at work within me.

I felt a strong urge to explore a different subject and, as I wandered through the library aisles, I found myself gravitating toward books on grief. I picked up book after book, carrying as many as I could, driven by an inner need to understand this profound topic.

I highlight the word grief because, even after twenty-five years, I still struggle with saying it. I've never liked that word, and I'm not sure I ever will. Stay with me, because later I do redefine it in a way that fosters growth beyond my experiences of loss, and helps me find light and meaning when I now navigate any form of loss.

It was a cool fall evening in October 2002, about four years after Danylo became an angel. The children—Larissa now nine years old and Adrian, two-and-a-half—and I had a regular nighttime routine: after supper, it was homework for her, a little television, bath, and bedtime stories. I tucked them lovingly into their warm beds, turned off their lights, and soon they were fast asleep. Their father was working abroad in the beautiful city of Paris and I found myself alone, but not lonely, in a space where I started what would end up being the most therapeutic grieving experience for me. I began to write.

I cleared the dining room table and opened the bag containing the heavy load of books. I placed them one by one on the table. Next to the books was a fresh comforting box of facial tissues that would capture the endless tears which rolled down my face as I put my words on paper. For five days straight that week, it was the same routine. Every night—with no interruptions—I read, I wrote, and I cried until I finished writing the draft of my paper. *Life… After the loss of a child* was done and ready to put in an academic format.

Over the next few weeks, I edited it, added the bibliography and endnotes, and included the articles.   On December 10, 2002, enclosed in a baby-blue front and back cover, I handed my paper, my story, my emotions, my pain, my grief, my life's story, to Professor Antonio Bernardelli.

It wasn't long before I got the paper back, a week before the Christmas break. Professor Bernardelli was one of those unforgettable professors, not only in his delivery of the course, but also in his amazing ability to keep us engaged and entertained with his stories. He took great pride in his role as a professor. The best part was that he was quick at providing his students with feedback. Who doesn't love that?

The papers were being handed out. One by one we were called up. I finally heard my name. Nervously, I went to the front of the room and Professor Bernardelli handed me my paper. Not only did it earn me one of the highest grades of all my work to that point, but my emotional journey was also validated when he said, "Tania, this is one of the most poignant papers I have ever read."

Those words and my story would often resurface in my life and, twenty years later, in one of the most unexpected and profound ways.

My master's degree, like my undergraduate degree, took me longer than it did for most students. It took six years to complete when the usual timeframe is two to three years…but who's counting? I wasn't. Once again, I was doing it part-time while still working full-time. It's funny — I've spent most of my career in higher education, yet because the university is also my workplace, I've never really experienced what it feels like to be a full-time student. How interesting is that?

It's important to find environments where you can leverage your talents and skills, but also continue to grow personally and professionally — places where you can nourish your life aspirations and make the most of the resources available.

For me, that place was higher education. Being a part-time student is certainly a different experience from being a full-time one. Campus life just isn't the same. Even so, my reality was that I was there day and night. Everything was integrated — it was a place to learn and an environment that fostered curiosity. I embraced every bit of knowledge that came from working, studying, and living life at McGill. I knew what I wanted and where I needed to be to get there.

A few years into my degree, in my Family Life and Marriage course, we explored relational patterns. One of our tasks was to create a three-generation genogram to examine the behavioral patterns in our own families.

Wow, this was quite the assignment! For me, it was challenging in the sense that I only really had my mother as a resource of information regarding my grandparents on both sides. Naturally she had more information to share about her side of the family and less about my father's side, but her memory was vivid. From her account, I was able to gain valuable information from my father's side, the Chomyks, as my father was no longer with us to share it from his perspective. I relied heavily on my mother's insights and those of a few distant cousins.

Interestingly, the professor in this course was none other than Professor Bernardelli. He taught several of the courses in this program. I was so happy. I loved him!

I started by chronologizing events and other significant facts related to our family for the period from 1919 until 2005. One of the first few things

I learned brought a huge smile to my face and soul. My great-grandmother, Eustyna Lysak from Luzok, Starij Sambir, Ukraine, was highly regarded in her village and considered as "the lady with the golden touch"—a woman capable of healing the sick. I felt this helped explain the strength and resilience of the women in my family, traits that have transcended down to my very own mother.

Just the image of my great-grandmother healing people, her face aglow, brought me tremendous pride—knowing she had this quality and the power to help and heal others. This is a quality that would permeate in our ancestral blood and shows itself still today.

I so wish I had met her. I wish I could have met my grandparents, but they both passed away at the age of sixty-three, before I was even born. I wonder if they know I exist.

As for my father's parents, I wish I had the opportunity to visit them in Ukraine before he and they passed away.

Our family, which was quite large, has now diminished so much that, apart from my cousins and second cousins, my mother at the age of ninety is the last survivor of her family of seven siblings. There are no more survivors from my father's immediate family of four brothers. It is so sad.

The exercise was a huge awakening for me in understanding that relational patterns exist within my family, as they do in all families. Whether we like it or not, history repeats itself but, I was only able to really appreciate and see that clearly, when I created the genogram.

What a gift it was to be able to put my entire family on a map. Even if I did not have all the pieces and dates, at least I have a picture of three generations that I can share with my own children…and them, with theirs.

But the real gift was not in the picture, it was in the insight that I gained, the "a-ha moment" I acquired once I was able to look at this map from outside in.

Critical events, patterns of alcohol dependency, mental health issues, and conflictual relationships stared me right in the face. It was irrelevant whether I had or had not met my relatives, I saw how patterns were perpetuated through the generations. I also knew that I could not stop or the change behaviors, let alone begin to understand another's struggle or the deep pain that drives someone to lean into alcohol.

That saddened me more than anything. I could only wish that my great-grandmother was alive so I could watch her heal their pain and take away their anxiety and sadness, but deep down I knew she could not…and neither could I. And in that pivotal moment, the only thing I could do was acknowledge what is and make a conscious decision to break the pattern for the sake of my children, and for myself.

I felt no animosity, no blame, no anger, or resentment—I just realized that this was my reality and nothing would change that unless I did. If I wanted to breathe peace and harmony back into my life, I had to make a shift in a new direction. That was the only thing I had the power to do. And so, I decided I would.

What a revelation! Who would have thought that this profound insight would become the catalyst for the change I was ready to make? By adopting an outsider's perspective and examining the evidence impartially, I was able to clearly see what was happening. Deep down, I knew this environment wasn't healthy for any of us and, despite my efforts to preserve the family, I began to question: Is this really worth preserving? And who am I preserving it for—others, society, or the community?

Ultimately, I realized that it wasn't any of those.

I pondered that insight for a while. It needed to settle within me. I needed time to process it and to see how my life would unfold given this newfound discovery. Always hopeful that things would change, despite knowing that the change would have to come from me, I held on.

The seed was planted. Movement began. I took to walking on a regular basis. Connecting with nature helped me escape my reality and provided me with the strength and peace of mind that would eventually become my instruments to act on when the time was right.

It was time. Provoked by an unexpected trigger, I made a decision that propelled me to take action toward a new direction in my life. This profound trigger came on a hot summer night almost two years after my insight.

It was an ordinary weekday in August 2008…or so I thought. But from the very start, something felt off. His return from the trip lacked its usual oomph, the energy in the house was rather muted, strange even. There was a tension I couldn't quite place, but I chose to push it aside. He was tired and went to sleep. I unplugged the phone in the bedroom so he could rest without distraction. Shortly after, I left the house and took Adrian to the mall to buy him some new shorts. I tried to go about the day as if nothing was wrong.

Within an hour or so, I received a text message from my daughter. Just a few words, but enough to unsettle me. Her father woke up abruptly and seemed to be frantically searching for the phone. My daughter, who was fifteen at the time and preparing for a synchro event, was in distress. My heart raced as I rushed back home, a growing sense of urgency tightening its grip on me.

When I reached her room, the sight of her stopped me in my tracks. She sat in the middle of her bed sobbing. Tears rolled down her face and her small frame trembled with fear. She looked so fragile and lost.

In that moment, something inside me broke—like a dam bursting under the weight of everything I had tried to ignore. Her distress was an accumulation of her nerves; it was not just related this one time. Her anxiety, her fear, struck me to my core. It was if her pain was reaching deep into my soul.

And then, as if a fog lifted, I saw it all with painful clarity. This moment, raw and unrelenting, was the wake-up call I could no longer avoid. The truth was undeniable: It was time to act. It was time to change. It was time to break free from the pattern and rewrite the story we were living.

I held her close, and in that embrace, I made a silent vow to her and to myself. No more. This was the beginning of something new and, for me, there was no going back—only forward.

That was the moment our lives truly began to shift. The moment I realized we were stepping into a new chapter—one I would never let us turn away from. One of peace, comfort, and stability.

It is remarkable how a single moment can act as a spark, igniting a decision that changes everything. The signs had always been there—the quiet brewing of tension, the subtle unease I ignored, and the fear of facing the unknown—but that one moment was the breaking point. It shattered the illusion I had clung to and propelled me forward, forcing me to confront the truth I had been too afraid to see.

Once again, it was my daughter—my unwavering rock—who became my catalyst for change. Her strength, even in the face of so much anxiety and uncertainty, reminded me of what truly mattered. Yet she wasn't the only one guiding me. Adrian, just eight years old at the time, showed me through his behaviors that he too needed to be free. Free from an environment that weighed on us all. And my angel in heaven was there too. I could feel his presence, steady and sure, pushing me forward with love and silent encouragement. My children were my force, the reason behind my actions, the ones who gave me the courage to break free. They showed me the way.

And quietly, my mother was there too. She supported me in her own way—ready to help once I made the decision, even before I found the words. Of course, she knew. She had experienced something similar. She and my father had separated, but without the formalities of divorce. They had agreed on an arrangement that had worked for them—he still came to the house regularly and, in many ways, their lives remained intertwined. It wasn't a traditional path, but it was one rooted in mutual respect and quiet understanding.

My path was different. I chose divorce—final and public. But, unlike my parents, we struggled to create the same level of amicability. It wasn't as graceful or as contained, but it was my truth and my mother honored that. Now, looking back through the lens of experience, I can see what I couldn't as a child: the strength it took for her to navigate her own choices, and the grace with which she held space for mine.

It wasn't just about leaving one life; it was about creating another—a life where freedom and peace weren't just a dream but a reality. The notion of freedom runs deep in my blood, threaded through my roots, carried by generations who fought to claim it. My family's journey to freedom is more than a history; it is a path laid out long before me and one I am now determined to honor. That was my moment to step onto that path, to rewrite our story, and to ensure that the legacy of resilience and hope continues with us.

JOURNEY TO FREEDOM

Breaking Ancestral Chains

Front row (from left to right): Second boy, my uncle Steve, age 6 (born 1939); third boy, my uncle Walter, age 5 (born 1940)—my mother's younger brothers.

Row behind the pole: Woman dressed in white with a kerchief, my grandmother Tetiana; to her left, my aunt Mary; and next to her, my mother, Rosalia, age 11.

ECHOES FROM THE PAST

We are our ancestors' wildest dreams.
Unknown

Tetiana, barefoot and terrified, fled Ukraine in a tattered dress, burying all her belongings in the backyard before escaping. The year was 1944, and Tetiana was my grandmother. The Russians were advancing, and survival meant leaving everything behind.

Just a year earlier, in 1943, the Germans had come to her village, claiming twenty-one-year-old boys to fight in the war. Desperate to protect her eldest son, Philip, my grandmother tried in vain to hide him. As he marched away from their home dressed in uniform, the village was consumed with the sounds of mothers screaming and crying, their hearts breaking under the weight of unimaginable loss.

Philip was more than just an eldest son; he was a beacon of love and strength for his family and community, always ready to lend a helping hand, especially to the elders. It came as no surprise when he received a medal of honor for saving lives in the first aid barracks, where he bandaged and healed bloodied soldiers.

For years, my grandmother clung to hope that Philip would return. His remains were never found so all she had were memories and the stories shared by Mr. Lazor, the last survivor to see Philip alive. Mr. Lazor somehow found his way to our community and was able to recount tales of Philip's bravery—how my uncle nursed wounded soldiers, saved lives, and ultimately saved *his* life. When the first aid barracks were destroyed by a bomb, Philip perished. But because of him, Mr. Lazor was spared and granted freedom. Until his recent passing, Mr. Lazor remained forever grateful to my uncle Philip, who not only saved him but also led him to a new life.

Even now, my mother cries every time she speaks of her eldest brother. "Tania," she says, her voice heavy with sorrow, "not even his medal was recovered."

For years, they hoped and prayed he would walk through the door. But he never came back.

Just last week, she shared a dream with me—one that seemed to bring both comfort and confirmation. In it, she and her mother were in the clouds, searching for her brother, longing to find some trace of him. As they wandered, Mother Mary appeared before them and spoke softly, yet firmly: "*Don't look for him. You will never find him.*"

That dream echoed a painful reality. When Ukrainian war veterans who had immigrated to Canada returned to the war-torn grounds in Europe to search for remnants of the fallen, they found medals—precious fragments of others who had been lost. But not Philips. Not even that. It was as if the Earth itself had swallowed every last trace of him, leaving only memories and an ache that never faded.

Tragedy struck again when my aunt Eustyna, separated from the family during their escape, returned to their abandoned home to search for them. She was found beaten to death near the apple tree in their yard. That news turned my grandmother's hair white overnight.

My grandmother's purpose became clear: To survive the war, protect her family, and provide shelter and food, no matter what the cost. Through months and years of uncertainty, the family traveled by wagon and train through Czechoslovakia and into Germany, where they would eventually live in camps. My grandmother almost missed the train once, frantically searching for food for her children. "Mama, hurry! Come back, please!" they cried in Ukrainian as the train began to move. She made it—always a fighter, always a survivor.

Through every tragic loss—her children, her home, her country—my grandmother carried an unshakable sense of hope and gratitude. She was thankful for every crumb, for the smallest kindnesses, and she believed deeply in paying it forward.

In the German camps, my two young uncles, blessed with beautiful voices, would sing as they wandered. People gathered to listen, and one older man, touched by their songs, would quietly leave a few potatoes or a piece of bread by their tent. My grandmother noticed his kindness. One day, she gathered food she had saved for her own children, tucked it into her apron, and brought it to the old man in gratitude. That was the kind of woman she was—a giver, a nurturer, a protector, and a healer.

These qualities are her legacy, woven into the fabric of the women in my family. I am proud to carry her name and the strength she embodied.

"We are rich," my late grandfather would say each day. These words echo through my mind, a remarkable mentality shaped by hardship yet filled with so much gratitude. And it is the mentality my mother inherited—a legacy born from having next to nothing but finding happiness in the simplest of things.

Imagine a childhood where one dress was all you owned—a dress patched, soaked, and stained, yet somehow cleansed by the splash of nearby water and the warmth of the sun or a crackling fire. This was my mother's reality, where potatoes and cabbage were their regular meal, and the occasional treat of latkes was a reason to celebrate. Meat was a luxury reserved for rare occasions, often only when a cow passed naturally, for in their eyes, cows were not just beef, but cherished companions.

Honorka—the name of their beloved cow—was a faithful companion during their difficult journey from Ukraine to Czechoslovakia. Leaving her behind was heart-wrenching, especially for my grandmother, who felt Honorka's sorrow in every tearful bellow. My grandmother visited her a few more times before embarking on the journey to Canada, each farewell heavier than the last. The memory of her abandonment is a poignant testament to the bond they shared, a reminder that true wealth is not measured by possessions, but by love, connection, and the stories we carry forward.

In 1949, after the war ended, Germany began arranging immigration contracts to Canada and North America. My aunt Mary, the eldest and now of age, was the first in our family to make the journey. She left alone, courageously embarking on a new chapter, knowing she would pave the way for the rest of her family. She found work as a domestic helper for a family in LaSalle, Montreal, Quebec, and quickly connected with *Prosvita*, a Ukrainian organization that would aid her in preparing the necessary papers to bring her family to Canada.

Next, it was my mother's turn to make the journey—again, alone, as families were not permitted to travel together in groups of more than two. She was just sixteen years old, but her age was falsified in her papers to show she was eighteen. My grandmother dressed her in her own worn clothes and handed her an old pair of boots to make her appear older. Somehow, it worked. My mother passed through and reunited with her sister in Canada. Together, they worked tirelessly, navigating complex processes and paperwork to ensure the rest of the family could join them.

In 1950, their determination paid off. My grandparents, along with their two youngest sons, finally arrived on Canadian soil. At long last, they were reunited—a family whole again, bound not only by blood but also by the gratitude of having survived, of being free to begin anew. They embraced their new life with open hearts, thankful for every opportunity this fresh start afforded them.

Throughout the years, my mother, Rosie, carried the lessons of strength, courage, and resilience learned from her own mother. Despite living with few necessities, my parents worked hard to build a happy, loving home for us within the vibrant Montreal Ukrainian community. My mother cherished the choices she had—choices her mother could never have imagined.

Yet, her own life was not without loss. As a young mother, she endured the pain of losing both her parents by the time they were sixty-three. They each died of strokes, conditions untreatable in those days. It is a bittersweet irony that today, in her ninety-first year, my mother lives with the same condition, managed with modern medicine.

As the youngest in my family, I never had the privilege of meeting my grandparents—or of them meeting me—yet their legacy has shaped my life in profound ways. When my mother discovered she was pregnant with her fourth child—me—she was deeply anxious. My father had lost his job, and my mother was already working tirelessly cleaning houses to feed their three children. How would they possibly manage a fourth?

It was Dr. Tarasczuk who offered her reassurance, saying in Ukrainian: "Rusia, I delivered your first three, and I will deliver this one. Mark my words, this child will make you the proudest."

While those words stay with me, I know in my heart that my mother is proud of each of us in her own way. My sister and brothers had carved their own meaningful paths and, together, we each reflect different pieces of her love, values, and legacy.

I was born on August 28, 1965, and named Tetiana, after my grandmother. Though I never knew her in life, I have always felt deeply connected to her—not just through her name, but through the values she embodied. She was the healer, the giver, the nurturer, and the protector. Those traits, so central to who she was, live on in me. They guide me as I strive to live a life of purpose, rooted in hope and gratitude, embracing the values instilled in me before I was even born.

Through her, I understand what it means to carry forward a legacy. It is not just about honoring the past, but also about embodying it—living it out every day, and ensuring it inspires those who come next. In my family, freedom was not just a gift, it was a hard-fought and deeply cherished achievement. And because of the sacrifices of those who came before me, I have had the privilege to live that freedom in the fullest and most meaningful way possible.

THE STRENGTH OF TOGETHERNESS

Alone, we can do so little; together, we can do so much.
Helen Keller

Coming to a foreign country doesn't feel as foreign when you can associate with your own kind. My mother found a sense of belonging in Canada by connecting with the Ukrainian community and Canadian cultures. She nourished her soul by helping the community—working in the church kitchen, giving talks and speeches at events, creating masterpiece fruit arrangements (she became known as an expert decorator), and welcoming new parishioners and all kinds of people into the community so openly and lovingly.

My mother always remaining true to who she is and was fully committed to our family, but she did relish all the accolades and appreciation she received for all her efforts. She found her purpose and her voice in giving back, in extending her love for her family to others. I believe that even until today, at the age of ninety-one, this is what continues to feed her soul, keeping her young and active in the community. Despite having lost so many of her friends and her dearest sister over the past few years, she remains engaged, involved, and interested in giving back to her parish and community in any way she can. That is her purpose for living.

A need for community has permeated into my own beliefs and guided my own immersion into one. I found my first love, the father of my children, by relishing all that my community brought me at that time and still today. More than belonging to a community, I believe we need to belong to ourselves. As Maya Angelou said: "You are only free when you realize you belong no place—you belong every place—no place at all. The price is high. The reward is great."

My mother's journey gave me the opportunity grow up in a free country—which was not her experience. Actually, in her own world, she probably did—she told me that, as a young child, she always felt free to play, learn, and be curious in everything she did. I can so relate because I too was raised in an environment that allowed me to be me—a dreamer, a believer, and an achiever. I was able to make my own choices without judgement or fear, and knew that I would be supported in any decision I made. Not everyone gets to experience this.

I am aware of that from my friends' childhood recollections, and from working with students who often feel that they do not have the choice to decide what they want to study or do. This saddens me because, deep down, I know that when we are not free to choose what we want to do, we are not being true to ourselves. And living someone else's truth goes against our inner peace, which creates conflict and challenges within. In this way, I truly feel I was one of the lucky ones.

Have you ever paused to consider the sacrifices that were made so you could choose your own path?

I am grateful to my mother and grandmother for showing me the way. What they sacrificed to come to Canada—their home, all of their belongings, and their community. Imagine leaving your home with nothing but each other. That was all that mattered. No shoes, no clothes—wearing the same dress for months. And yet, she smiles—she always smiles and always finds the good in everything. Because when you appreciate having that one potato or eating a fresh apple from a garden, you have it all. When you have space to run and play, to sing and dance, with your surviving siblings—without any other worries in the world—yes, you have it all.

Free-spirited and happy, I get it from my mother. Her divergent mind, and her interest in everything that sparked an energy in her as she discovered and embraced all her talents—singing, reciting poems, giving speeches, organizing church events, leading the kitchen ladies, learning to create masterful fruit designs for weddings, catering…just to name a few. She always says to me, "Tania, with all my stories I could write a book." And, despite not having any formal education, she can…in Ukrainian. Every day she writes in her calendar about what she did and what made her happy. She is ninety years old and has years of calendars filled with this information. So, in reality, she has written a book—perhaps not formally, but in her own way. I am so proud to be able to take that dream, that desire of hers, and write this book—not only for me, but also for her, and for all who will benefit from her wisdom, our collective wisdom through our life's journey, with blissfully beautiful moments and poignantly painful ones.

I never had the chance to meet my grandmother, Tetiana, but my mother made sure I felt like I did. Growing up, I often wondered: *Why don't I have a grandmother like the other kids?* Somehow, my mother found a way to answer that question. She introduced me to Pani—Ms. Malashka—a kind and sturdy woman from our church, known for her humble heart and quiet dedication to serving the Ukrainian community.

Pani Malashka lived alone in a small, cozy home nearby. She had never married nor had children of her own. She was a pillar in our church, always the first to lend a hand or make a journey to visit others, her heart full of generosity. And, in the way that only a grandmother could, she wrapped me in her embrace, sharing her warmth through big hugs, little gifts, and even the occasional piece of chocolate or a dollar. For a while, I felt as though I, too, had a grandmother.

As I grew older, I learned the beautiful truth: It was my mother who had given Pani Malashka those chocolates and coins to share with me, orchestrating each moment so I could experience the love of a grandmother. Her love was the foundation, the quiet force creating a world where I never felt a void. She knew the gift she was giving me wasn't just sweets or pocket money—it was the magic of belonging, of feeling cherished.

Looking back now, I wonder if Pani Malashka was more than just a stand-in. Perhaps she was, in some way, my grandmother Tetiana reaching across time and spirit, slipping into this kind woman's 'Earth suit,' to hold me one more time, carrying the love through the generations.

More and more, I hear people say, "You are your mother's daughter," and while that is true in so many ways, I have come to realize just how much I've evolved away from her way of thinking. In our own unique ways, we both love to give. For my mother, that giving often comes with a need for perfection—her way, or no way. Growing up, I felt that weight, that expectation that everything needed to be just right. It was a pattern I inherited.

My mother always emphasized appearance—how we dressed for church or Ukrainian school. Image was important, and I get that now, but over time I've evolved. I have learned that it's okay if I don't 'fancy up' for church. What matters is my presence, my intention to pray. I no longer feel bound by the need to meet an image or standard. I have come to understand that it's okay if others do things their own way too.

For my mother, it was often 'her way or the highway'—a mindset that didn't always leave room for others to be free. That is something I struggled with growing up. For a long time, I tried to control everything around me, believing that perfection would bring peace. But through my own growth, I have come to realize that true peace comes from letting go of control and embracing life as it flows. This shift didn't happen overnight—it's a lesson that took years to learn, and it's a gift I carry with me today...a blend of her teachings and my own evolution.

This lesson, this journey of change, is something I carry with me: *Let me be me, and you be you.*

I have learned to let go, to ignore the urge to correct, and to resist engaging in that dialogue. But I have also come to understand a deeper truth: many times, my need to guide or suggest was rooted in protecting my own expectations. I wanted to shield myself from disappointment, to ensure things went a certain way so I wouldn't feel let down. Recognizing this has been humbling, and it's taught me to lower my expectations—not of her, but of my need for control— and to simply let her be.

Take Christmas, for example. Growing up, Christmas meant perfection— everything ironed, shoes shiny, appearances just right. My mother's iron was always busy, smoothing out every crease, every wrinkle, ensuring everything was flawless. Today, I hardly ever touch an iron unless absolutely necessary… proof of how far I've come(?).

One year, my daughter showed up to our Christmas gathering dressed how she wanted—casual and comfortable. I had so much to say, but I stopped myself. What was I doing? She was happy and, in that moment, she showed me that it didn't matter what she wore. What mattered most was just being together as a family and enjoying the celebrations. Lesson learned.

Over time, that's exactly how our Christmas has evolved. Cozy and comfy, no frills, no pressure—just the flickering, twinkling lights of candles at the dinner table, and the one we light for our angels, for our ancestors who have passed. It is a tradition that feels so much more meaningful, a reflection of the peace and freedom I've been working to embrace.

Of course, as a mother, it is hard to resist offering suggestions now and then. But I've been working hard to make it less about me and more about my children. I catch myself in those moments when I want to tell my daughter what to wear or how to behave, and I pause. I remind myself that this is her journey, not mine. Instead of imposing my preferences, I'm learning to trust her choices and give her the freedom to grow into herself.

Living so close to my mother, I see more and more how much I emulate her — yet I also see how far I've moved away from her way of thinking. We may not share the same roof, but the apple didn't fall far from the tree. Still, what I've learned and who I've become is uniquely my own.

I often think about my oldest brother, Walter, who was ten years older than me. As I grew into adulthood, our age gap began to feel smaller, and I was inching toward his level. Sadly, Walter left us all too soon. I know Walter is close, watching over us with my son and my father. I miss him deeply and wish I'd had more time to share those moments that could have brought us closer. It's funny, though, how much of him I still see in myself—the oldest and the youngest, yet somehow cast from the same mold.

Walter and I shared a love for reading: he loved fiction, while I lean toward nonfiction. He was a linguist, fluent in five languages, while I know three and dabble in a few others. He had a deep, quiet intellect, a love for learning that I share. We would have had such incredible conversations. Walter was content with a simple life—a job, a home, and family—and perhaps he felt he didn't quite fit in. Despite becoming a father at a young age, he never fully embraced family life. Yet, as time passes, I feel his absence more deeply and his presence more profoundly, guiding me alongside my son and father. Together, they inspire me every day, fueling my journey and motivating me as I write this book.

I feel their presence, and throughout the years I have gained an appreciation of who Walter was—a bit of a loner and introvert, which I can relate to. Today, I understand how he saw the world, and I wish I'd had that insight back then. I imagine the conversations we'd have now, the wisdom I could share with him, and he with me.

So, *my dearest brother Walter, even though I cannot speak to you here, I hope you can hear me when I say, I love you, and I know you are guiding me from above.*

Walter my brother, Tato my father, and Danylo my son, I feel you at my side in the moments I need you most—when I feel drained, out of sorts, and disconnected. I know you see me pull back and retreat into my cocoon, wanting nothing but solitude, but I know you understand. And, in those quiet moments, you reach into my heart, remind me of the light within, and urge me to move forward.

And I am. Each and every day.

WHAT IS TRUE FREEDOM?

Freedom lies in being bold.
Robert Frost

When I think of freedom, it's about knowing you have a choice in everything you say or do. I firmly believe that we all have a choice in how we think, how we react, and how we show up in any situation. That is where we hold our power.

Our thoughts may stream into our minds uninvited, but we ultimately decide how those thoughts will manifest in our actions. What power will we give them? How will we choose to express them?

Responsibility lies within us. When we do something—or nothing—about a situation, we are making a choice. It is not about being passive in the face of life's challenges; it's about actively deciding how we want to approach them. And no-one, no circumstance, can take that power away from us. As Viktor Frankl so eloquently put it, "Everything can be taken from a man but one thing: the last of human freedoms—to choose one's attitude in any given set of circumstances, to choose one's own way."

This philosophy has been woven into the fabric of who I am. No matter how difficult life has been, no matter what has been thrown my way, I've always known—deep down—that I have a choice. How I respond, how I move forward, that is what I own. That is the freedom I can never lose. It is something we all own, if we are willing to claim it.

I choose not to place the blame on anyone else for my decisions. I made that choice, that commitment, years ago, but it was after the passing of Danylo that I truly learned the depth of that choice. In those dark, heavy days after losing him, I had to choose between peace and dysfunction, love and hate. I realized that the decision was mine to make and that nobody, no event, could take it from me.

Throughout my marriage, preserving our family unit was the most important thing for me. Seeing the glass as half-full—believing that good was always there—was how I got through the ups and downs of life. We had beautiful moments, made happy memories, and were blessed with three miracles. The birth of our second son, Adrian, was a profound gift which filled a void, renewed the essence of our 'million-dollar family', and, for a while at least, coated over the deeper, underlying issues that had yet to fully resurface.

But here's the thing about problems and issues—they don't go away unless we deal with them. I could have kept ignoring them, kept them locked away from the world, but that would have been living in denial. It was like living inside a bubble—safe and protected, but ultimately unsustainable. Eventually, that bubble burst.

Everything happens in its own time. I believe we live the life we are meant to live, exactly as it unfolds. My thirst for knowledge and my drive for continuous learning brought me insights I could not have imagined. As I pursued my master's degree, I learned a new language and was given new tools to understand mental health, alcohol dependency, grief, and all the hidden complexities of life—my life. Through my studies, I learned about loss, failure, and abuse, and gained an awareness of the generational patterns that run through my family.

At first, I only saw bits and pieces of the environment I had lived in, but as I learned, my understanding deepened. I began to see my life from a wider, more objective perspective. And what I saw no longer offered the peace, the happiness, and the freedom I so desperately needed, craved, and yearned for. Like my mother, I had always chosen to see the good, the silver lining, the bigger picture. And, for the longest time, that worked. I protected the family unit that I so cherished but, by constantly discounting the dysfunction around me, I sheltered our reality from the harsh light of truth, until I could no longer ignore it.

My ability to compartmentalize became my tool for survival. It surfaced when uncomfortable situations arose, allowing me to block out the chaos when it felt too overwhelming. I rarely feared for my physical safety and I knew that the emotional turmoil was temporary. The bark was worse than the bite, so to speak. It was like I had an unshakable confidence that everything would be okay—that the storm would pass. I trusted that the words, the outbursts, the shouting would eventually give way to apologies, flowers, and tears. Until the next time.

But the truth is, that cycle was not freedom. It was survival, a mechanism to hold things together when the pieces were coming undone. It wasn't until I began to embrace the choice within me—the choice to break free from old patterns—that I began to understand what true freedom really means.

True freedom does not come from avoiding pain, or from pretending that everything is okay when it's not. It comes from facing the hard truths, from embracing the full spectrum of emotions, and from choosing how to move forward in a way that honors who we are and who we are becoming. Freedom is the ability to choose, to act with intention, and to make peace with the parts of ourselves we've been hiding or running from.

And that—that is the real freedom I now see and understand: It's about owning our power to choose how we respond, no matter what life presents. It's about finding the courage to stop surviving, and to start living with purpose. And it's the most empowering freedom we can ever claim.

WHEN HISTORY REPEATS

History, despite its wrenching pain, cannot be unlived,
but if faced with courage, need not be lived again.
Maya Angelou

As a little girl, I remember occasions when there was shouting, anger, and alcohol in our home. In fact, the shouting and anger only ever surfaced when alcohol mixed with jealousy. Earlier in my adult life, I seldom spoke about those moments that brought my family and me such discomfort, because I couldn't reconcile those memories with my loving father. I didn't want to remember anything other than the happy moments that filled my childhood with joy and laughter — and there were plenty more of those.

Playing school, going to the park with my dad, having all kinds of pets — chickens, a rabbit, fish, frogs, and a cat — learning to paint Ukrainian Easter eggs, taking part in church plays, singing and dancing with my siblings, traveling with my scout friends, performing, and embracing our Ukrainian culture in every possible way — that was what my life looked like most of the time.

My mother, the leader of my two parents, showed us what it meant to belong to a community, to value family, traditions, and culture, and to embrace our talents. My father, on the other hand, was the one who carried me on rainy days so my feet wouldn't get wet. He signed my failed tests so Mom wouldn't know. He made my lunches while I watched *The Flintstones* on school days and always let me keep the change when he sent me to the store. He was, and will always be, my silent hero.

I inherited my father's sensitivity and his way of being — always protective of his family. He never compared himself to anyone; he simply did not care. That's what I admired most about him. He was the humblest person I knew and appreciated every single little thing he had. Like my mother, he loved his family. We were his everything.

But what a life he had.

Being the second of four boys and seen as the daughter my grandmother never had, my father stayed behind to help his mother in the house. He was so compassionate and caring, and he actually enjoyed housework. He didn't have a complaining bone in his body.

Imagine, at the age of eighteen, having to dig graves for dead soldiers during World War II. How could that not affect a person?

His Post-traumatic stress disorder (PTSD) eventually caused difficulties in my parents' marriage and home life for all of us became harder. In fact, the issues started earlier, during their courtship—like it had for in my marriage. But, like her daughter years later, my mother ignored the signs and thought nothing of it. It is good that she did, because otherwise I would not be here today to share this story with others. We were meant to live this life.

My father struggled with jealousy and, combined with his drinking, this became a bigger problem for my parents and our family. To my father, my mother was his everything. Like the potato he once procured back in Ukraine when he trespassed gardens to bring food home to his family, he held on to her for dear life. Sharing her with others was hard for him to digest. My mother, however, needed more—she needed recognition and a greater sense of belonging, both within herself and within her community. She needed and wanted more. That created problems in their marriage.

There was no communication or sharing of one's feelings or needs; it simply wasn't something my parents did. Who talked about their needs, their desires, their wants, anyway? Certainly not in those days. No one knew how to address those issues. Who would? They were not formally educated, and, besides, who didn't have mental health issues? They did, as did all the generations before them. We just didn't know how to talk about it, so we did our best to live with it.

For years, I believed I had inherited my father's sensitivity—his open-hearted tears at sad events or touching stories, the way he wore his emotions on his sleeve. But, as I explored the meaning of sensitivity, trauma, and emotions more deeply, I realized something profound: I had inherited this trait from both of my parents. My father just expressed his sensitivity outwardly, while my mother held hers deep within.

Sensitivity is often misunderstood. It's not just about shedding tears or showing emotion, it's about allowing yourself to feel deeply. It's the ability to sense the subtle undercurrents of life—the pain, the joy, the heartbreak, the hope—and carry it all within you. This can manifest in different ways: through the tears that fall freely, or through the silence and stoicism that hold emotions at bay. Both are forms of strength, and both tell stories about the weight of what we carry and the ways we protect ourselves.

For much of her life, my mother appeared stoic, her tears hidden behind a shield of resilience. She had shed so many in her younger years that it was as though her body had run out of them. Her grief was buried under layers of armor, forged by an early tragedy that left scars too deep to show. She never really cried—not in front of us, not in front of anyone. And yet, as she grows older, the floodgates are re-opening. Now in her nineties, whenever she recounts stories of her family, her brothers, and the war in Ukraine, her tears flow freely. The shield is gone, and with it, the guard she held up for so many years.

This contrast between my parents helped me reflect on my own relationship with sensitivity. I see now that I live in a space between them, embodying both their ways of feeling and protecting. I cry easily, just like my father did, and those moments often come unexpectedly—triggered by a story, a memory, or even the beauty of a fleeting moment. But, like my mother, I've also learned to put up a shield when the weight of the world feels too heavy to bear. There are days when my emotions feel too raw, and the only way to protect myself is to tuck them away, building walls to guard my heart.

This interchange between crying and shielding has become a dance—a delicate balance between vulnerability and strength. Crying is not a sign of weakness, it's a release, a way of honoring what is within. It's the body's natural response to the emotions we carry, a signal that we are alive and human. Yet there are times when we need the shield, not to deny our feelings but to hold them in until we feel ready to face them. My mother and father showed me that sensitivity exists on a spectrum and that both crying and shielding are valid ways of navigating life's complexities.

Crying is an expression of sensitivity, but so too is the quiet endurance of emotions that aren't ready to surface. Both are tied to trauma, which can heighten our sensitivity to the world around us. Trauma teaches us to protect ourselves, sometimes by keeping our emotions hidden, and sometimes by letting them spill out. It can shape how we cry, when we cry, or why we don't cry. But underneath it all, sensitivity remains—it's what connects us to our deepest truths.

I see now that sensitivity is not a single trait but a multifaceted one. It is the tears that fall and the strength it takes to hold them back. It is the armor we wear and the courage to take it off. It is the interplay of emotions, the ebb and flow of feeling deeply yet knowing when to protect our hearts.

Through this exploration, I've come to understand my parents in new ways. My father's sensitivity was raw and visible, my mother's restrained and buried. Yet both carried the weight of their emotions in ways that reflected their lives, their struggles, and their resilience. And in recognizing this, I've come to honor my own sensitivity—the way I navigate between crying and shielding, between feeling deeply and holding on.

My parent's stories have taught me that sensitivity is not just about how we express emotions but how we live with them. It's about finding strength in our tears and wisdom in our silence. And it's a reminder that our emotions, no matter how they show up, are a testament to our humanity, our courage, and our connection to the world around us.

I was devastated when I lost my father just before my thirtieth birthday—a loss that echoed the grief my mother felt when her parents had passed—but I do find some solace in knowing that he joined the angels in heaven three years before my son did. He was spared from witnessing the unbearable tragedy that unfolded: seeing his grandson, my Danylo, in a tiny baby-blue coffin at a funeral home meant for adults, not babies. Not his grandson.

And then there was my brother, Walter—his firstborn son. To lose both a grandson and a son is unthinkable, a tragedy unheard of in our community at the time. My only consolation is knowing that when Danylo arrived in heaven, he was welcomed with open arms by his grandfather(s)—men who would have adored him on Earth just as they now do in heaven.

When I reflect on my family's history, I see a lineage marked by tremendous loss, with each generation facing heartbreak. My grandmother Tetiana's greatest pain was losing her home and her homeland, but her deepest sorrow lay in the tragic deaths of her children—losses she was mostly spared from witnessing firsthand. She was with her fourth daughter, Anastasia, when she died at the age of three from what began as a bump under her arm and developed into a life-threatening disease. When her son Philip and her daughter Eustyna perished, she was far away and only learned of their fate through the stories of others. Yet, in her heart, she always held onto hope— hope that they might one day return, or that she would see them again in another life. It was this hope, this small but powerful flame, that kept her going, giving her a reason to live despite all she had lost.

My mother, too, has known unimaginable grief. She was there to live and carry the grief of her mother's pain, her daughter's pain, and her own.

Losing a child is devastating at any age. My mother and I have both had to face that unbearable pain. My son, Danylo, was taken from me, passing quietly in his sleep at just six months old. Within a year, my mother witnessed the final moments of my oldest brother, Walter. Holding his hand, she heard his last words, "Mummy, I love you,"—words that have echoed through her life, words she repeats almost every day.

These two losses, so close together, felt like too much to bear.

I remember thinking: *How could this be happening? To her, to him, to us?* It felt incomprehensible that God could take someone so young, leaving my nephew Stephan without his father who loved him so deeply.

History, it seems, has a cruel way of repeating itself. But while pain is inevitable, suffering is optional. It is a choice. We were not meant to be lifelong sufferers—instead, we are warriors of grief. God gives us what we can handle, and what we do with it is up to us. For me, the path forward is clear: I choose hope, resilience, and the desire to create better outcomes—not only for myself, but for others who walk this difficult road ahead.

On February 19, 2022, when Russia invaded Ukraine, our community couldn't believe what was happening. My mother and so many other survivors of World War ll, had to relive their history, albeit now from afar as they witnessed horrific scenes unfold on their television sets.

Fortunately, my mother, the last survivor of her family, was safe in Canada but she felt ever so helpless in what she could do. I will never forget the screech in her voice when she rang me in tears, *"Nasha Ukrainia Propadaye"*—our Ukraine is perishing.

It broke my heart to hear her pain. I could feel it. Although I had never experienced it, I felt her pain and connection to Ukraine. What horror! How could this be? How could one Russian ruler just decide to take over our Ukraine—a country that had fought for years for sovereignty which was finally granted in 1991? Sadly, deep down I always felt that Ukraine, one of the richest European countries, would never ever be left alone. Not by the Russians anyway.

Our Ukrainian community came together in an incredible show of solidarity, and our church opened its hall doors for months to support the influx of displaced immigrants. People from all over the city and beyond would stop by to donate medical supplies, baby food and products, clothes of all sizes, kitchen items, winter wear, and more. We worked together to prepare packages for the families arriving on Canadian soil, escaping the war and seeking a new life. Most of these new arrivals were women and children—husbands and fathers had stayed behind to fight the war.

Really? It is 2022, and yet war is repeating itself. I never imagined I would experience this, and neither did my mother. But, once again, history was repeating itself.

I felt a deep, overwhelming need to help in any way I could. So, I drove to the church and began sorting the endless boxes of donations that arrived by the minute, by the hour, by the day. The hall quickly became unrecognizable, filled with people and goods. Despite the gravity of the situation, we came together as a community to help however we could. The women in the kitchen began making pierogies and cabbage rolls to raise money for the families, and I found a role I could fill. I became in charge of marketing and selling dozens of pierogies and cabbage rolls to anyone who wanted to support the cause. Orders started pouring in. I set up a station under the church hall and, for the next few months, every Saturday I would be at the church—packing orders, collaborating with the kitchen team, and selling out of pierogies and cabbage rolls until there was nothing left. I didn't even need to post on social media, people found me, called me, and the orders kept coming in. My mother would be there every Saturday, helping in her own way, but more often observing as I took charge of the initiative…just as she would have back in her day.

Those women worked tirelessly, week after week, preparing food. I got to do what seemed like the easy part—selling—but in truth, we all played to our individual strengths and prevailed as a team. Together, in just a few months, we raised around twenty-seven-thousand-dollars to help support families in Ukraine. The feeling of uniting as one and making a difference was indescribable.

But that is what a community does. That is what was instilled in me. No-one had to tell me what to do. I simply found a way to contribute, to make the best of a challenging situation.

And now, two years later, who would have thought that I would be personally supporting newly arrived immigrants—including many from Ukraine—as they transition to life in Canada? Through my work at La Passerelle, a career transition service for mature professionals, and more prominently through the Career Planning course I teach at the School of Continuing Studies, I find myself exactly where I am meant to be. Reflecting on my parents' journey to Canada—how they offered their hands for blue-collar work, and how grateful they were for the opportunities in this land of freedom—I realize that these highly skilled, talented, and educated immigrants I am working with are just striving for the same thing. History has a way of repeating itself, but we have the power to shape it for the better.

The women in my class are a truly inspirational. Despite the challenges of navigating a system far more complex than the one my parents faced, they show me what resilience truly means. They are not only surviving—they are blossoming. Their hope, combined with their gratitude for being here, drives them forward every day. They remind me that, even in the face of hardship, their will to keep going is fueled by their belief in a better future. This, too, is what we have in common—the thread of my ancestry binds us. It is the spirit of resilience, hope, and an unyielding belief in a brighter tomorrow.

And, never giving up.

EMBRACING FREEDOM

Discovering Self and Values

A NEW PATH FORWARD

Your life does not get better by chance; it gets better by change.
Jim Rohn

From a young age, I sought refuge in a quiet space of my own—one where I could let my imagination roam freely and express my deepest thoughts. I created that space in the pages of a diary, a private world that brought me a sense of peace. Throughout my life, I've held onto that sacred place as a place where I can always return to find clarity and calm, even in the face of life's challenges.

Motion and rocking became my way to disconnect from the weight of the world around me. When I was a child, my siblings and I would sit on the living room floor and rock against the couch. It is something we started doing while listening to music. As I got older, I'd slip into my brother's room when he wasn't there to use his ghetto blaster and enjoy the comfort of his big chair. I'd lose myself to the rhythm, swaying back and forth to the sounds of Ukrainian melodies. This continued through my teenage years into adulthood as the sounds of Olivia Newton-John, Cher, Ricky Martin, Celine Dion, The Bee Gees, and a myriad of other artists, sang songs that seemed to relate to me and offer me comfort in ways I couldn't put into words then.

Even now, motion is a thread that brings me clarity and calm. I find the same solace in long walks and in the gentle sway of the swing on my balcony where I can immerse myself in a book or the soft hum of music. These rhythms are my sanctuary. They bring me back to that inner space of peace—a thread that's always guided me.

In 2016, while enrolled in my Personal and Professional Coaching Certification, I encountered a moment that took my inner clarity to a new level. In our final class, our professor introduced us to the Theory U model—an approach to leadership by Otto Scharmer that invites us to open our minds, hearts, and will. This model taught us a new way of being via a path to greater awareness that included the head's logic, the heart's intuition, and a grounded sense of purpose. We explored how embracing each of these parts of ourselves can lead to positive change—not only within us, but also in the communities and organizations we are part of. Our professor would often remind us, "You have to let go to start something new."

Guided by this principle, we were encouraged to take ten slow steps around the room, close our eyes, and envision our future as we waited for a door or gate to appear. In my mind's eye, a vision unfolded. I saw myself as a six-year-old, running through a magical garden filled with vibrantly coloured flowers and fluttering butterflies—a space so open and joyful it felt like freedom itself. In that moment, I connected with the memory of living freely, purely, and with such bliss.

Then, another door appeared. This time, it was the entrance to the building where I worked. As I looked, an unsettling feeling washed over me. The image was clouded, and the familiar faces around me seemed distant, even empty. A powerful question formed within me: Is this a glimpse of what I needed to let go?

Without realizing it, this vision was guiding me toward a pivotal shift in my career and life. It was calling me to align my path with a vision of freedom I had long held in my heart, setting me on a journey of liberation both personally and professionally. This was the beginning of embracing a new chapter, one where I could live in harmony with the sense of freedom, I'd always been drawn to…the one I'd caught a glimpse of as a child but could now claim as my own.

Sometimes, however, I do find myself pondering the balance between my deep desire for freedom and the possibility of nurturing a new meaningful, loving relationship. Can I truly be independent while sharing my life with someone else?

That question lingers, a reminder of how essential it is to be true to ourselves first. We must honor our individuality before we embrace the role of partner, spouse, or parent. I believe this deeply—especially as I have seen many women lose themselves in identities they adopted after marriage. For me, freedom isn't just about space; it's about retaining the core of who I am, even as I open my life to others. And so, I've always made it a point to stay connected to my essence, to pursue the life I envision and remain true to what I want, while still finding space for love and connection along the way.

Having the right partner can make all the difference. When I was married, my friends would often say, "Oh, you went on vacation with your friends? He lets you do that?"

The fact is, when I celebrated my fortieth birthday, my husband generously funded a trip for me and my friends, reinforcing my belief that I *could* be my true self while still being a devoted partner and mother. For me, it all comes down to feeling secure in a relationship, and perhaps marriage brought a certain ease in navigating my need for independence—there was a foundation of trust, with no real threat.

Since my divorce, however, my relationships have highlighted the ongoing challenge of finding a balance between connection and the freedom I hold dear.

Marina Bryezhahova, a guest speaker for a Career Planning course I taught last summer, once said, *"Our values inflict a certain amount of pain."*

Her words resonated deeply with me, unveiling a truth I hadn't fully acknowledged: Freedom does have a cost, and my understanding of it won't always resonate with others, not even with a partner.

Ultimately, I know I need to live my truth. This isn't just a principle I hold dear, but one I teach in my 'Be the CEO of Your Career and Life' program. How can I not live what I impart to others?

And I've raised my children to honor their own authenticity, to understand that aligning with who they truly are is the key to fulfillment. This is the foundation I believe in. It is why I ask others—and myself: Are you showing up as who you really are? Do you feel that you can do that?

Because I know that, in the end, we all deserve to live as our most genuine selves.

Showing up as who you are and nurturing yourself can be challenging. Depending on the phase of life we find ourselves in, we will prioritize the needs of others over our own desires and goals. Certainly, there are moments when we must lean into our responsibilities—that is entirely natural. However, if we can consciously integrate the things that bring a sense of purpose and joy into our lives as we fulfill those responsibilities, then we can cultivate a deeper sense of contentment and alignment within ourselves. Ultimately, this inner happiness will then radiate outwards, enriching not only our life, but the lives of those around us.

Throughout my life, I've focused on finding ways to maintain my interests, pursue my goals, and honor my values while still striving to be the best daughter, sister, wife, partner, and mother I can be. As women, especially as mothers, we often juggle numerous responsibilities alongside an inherent need to care for our families—it is woven into our very nature. I embrace this reality and take pride in being a woman. In fact, I truly love it. Yet, I also recognize that preserving my identity is just as important, if not more so, than fulfilling these roles.

Even in moments when I feel stretched thin, I make a conscious effort to carve out time for 'Tania.' Whether it's meditating, taking a walk, diving into a good book, listening to music, sitting on my swing, or journaling, I know these moments of self-care are essential for my well-being. I understand what I need, and I am unafraid to seek it out.

However, lately I've noticed that balancing these various roles has become increasingly challenging. With an aging mother, it seems my responsibilities are increasing. As the only one of her children to live in the city, much of the caregiving and support for my mother has fallen on my shoulders. It is a profound shift that brings both joy and weight, and I am learning to navigate the new dynamic while still honoring my own needs.

It is not easy—neither on her nor on me. I am, however, grateful that she lives autonomously in a Ukrainian residence and doesn't require full-time care. For that, I consider myself, and her, fortunate. I know that the time will come when our roles may reverse, and in some ways, they already have. I see glimpses of her childlike nature reflected in my own, a trait I believe I inherited from her.

One of my statements in my credo is to remain childlike at heart. This essence of creativity and playfulness is something my mother embodied. I remember a story she shared from when she was a child picking up silver gum wrappers off the floor to make ornaments for Christmas—an activity I would gladly take part in. She had a remarkable talent for turning nothing into something beautiful. Her creativity truly flourished when she began catering in her late fifties alongside my Aunt Mary. It was Aunt Mary who invited her to help out one day and, from that moment on, my mother blossomed into one of the best fruit decorators in our community.

She took immense pride in her work, crafting stunning sweet tables for weddings, particularly within our Italian, Jewish, and Ukrainian communities. Not only did she revel in the artistry of her creations, but she also brought home the leftover fruits and goodies for us to enjoy—a testament to her caring nature. Just like her mother, my grandmother, who fed not just her family but anyone in need, my mother exemplified the nurturing spirit that has defined the women in our family for generations.

But her artistry didn't stop at sweet tables. She also crafted a breathtaking bridal crown, adorned with traditional Ukrainian flowers—poppies, sunflowers, and delicate blossoms—woven together with love. During our bridal showers, my sister and I each had the honor of standing beneath its beauty as its long ribbons cascaded across the stage, with blue and yellow at the forefront, a quiet tribute to our heritage.

That crown became more than just a decoration—it became a tradition. Mothers from our community borrowed it for their own daughters, passing it from one celebration to the next. It traveled through so many hands, a silent witness to love, union, and shared joy. And yet, today, it is nowhere to be found. No one knows exactly where it ended up, who last held it, or where it now rests.

And the remarkable thing? That doesn't bother my mother. It was never about keeping the crown, but about what it meant—the way her craftsmanship wove itself into the lives of others, the way her hands created something that became part of a greater story. That, more than anything, is her legacy.

The famous saying "we rise by lifting others" rings profoundly true for me. I have found that my own joy increases when I help others. The satisfaction I derive from giving and nurturing is immense. Gratitude, giving, and a spirit of service are the keys to a fulfilling life. I have learned that when you give, you receive—often in ways you might not expect. This mindset of living with abundance is deeply ingrained in my identity, as it was in my mother and grandmother, even in times of scarcity. They always found reasons to be grateful, and the more grateful they were, the more blessings seemed to flow into their lives.

Every day my mother thanks God for her life, for living in Canada, and for having everything she needs. She expresses gratitude for nature—the songs of birds and the warmth of the sun. As I reflect on this, I realize I share that same sense of appreciation. It is fascinating how, in my later years, I've come to see just how much we have in common. Have you ever paid attention to the similarities you see in your own life and those of your loved ones?

For me, one of the greatest gifts of gratitude is that it creates space to imagine, to dream, and to trust that we are exactly where we need to be. It opens the door to vision—a vision of what *is* possible, even when life feels uncertain. And vision, just like gratitude, invites us to look beyond the immediate and connect with something deeper: A future that reflects not only what we hope for, but also who we truly are.

This is where our journey into vision begins because, before we can see clearly what comes next, we must first recognize the dreams that already live within us.

VISION INTO REALITY

If you can imagine it, you can achieve it.
If you can dream it, you can become it.
William Arthur Ward

On a beautiful, hot summer's day in July 2023, I woke up and ventured outside for a walk-in nature. I had chosen to write this book in the countryside, just as I envisioned. I rented a cottage by the lake from a dear family friend—a place that has become a happy place for me, a space of calm, peace, and serenity. It is unbelievable how closely my reality mirrored the image I had pinned on my vision board, yet there I was, writing exactly where I imagined I would be, nurturing my mind, body, and soul. It was as if I *had* to be there.

Does that ever happen to you? Do you close your eyes and envision where you want to be, and how good it feels to do what you love, and then, in some mystical, magical way, it begins to unfold before your very eyes?

That is exactly what it felt like writing this book. The vision was clear, even the process. Taking the steps made me feel so much closer to realizing it, even though there were moments when I wondered: *Who am I to be writing a book?*

Clarity doesn't always mean the path will be smooth—and that's when you have to rely on your intuition and trust the process.

I did then and I do now.

In 2019, after I created my very first vision board, it became very obvious how unhappy I felt in my position at work. My energy was scattered, my motivation drained, and I often felt unwanted. I began to feel disengaged from my work and disconnected from the people around me. The community wasn't as vibrant as it once was, and I started feeling lonely and isolated. Something was up. I was tired of the bureaucracy and politics within the structure, and felt boxed into roles that no longer served me—to be honest, they never really had, I had just found ways to make them work. Over time, it became increasingly harder to bring my true self to work. Leadership changes altered the environment, and it was then that I began to understand *why* things felt so off.

Meanwhile, other areas of my life were lighting me up—especially after earning my coaching certification in 2017. All I wanted to do was inspire and empower others in a meaningful way…just as I had empowered myself. I felt called to help women take ownership of their careers and lives. That passion is what led me to create my 'Be the CEO of Your Career and Life' program which I launched in 2023.

However, please don't think that the solution to my work problems fell into place all at once. Many of my earlier actions and ideas resurfaced unexpectedly — as if they were part of a bigger plan. A business case I had once pitched to my supervisor, for example, became the groundwork for the freedom I craved.

I had already begun to see myself as an entrepreneur, free from the constraints of an organization — something clearly reflected on my vision board. It was as if the Theory U exercise I did in my coaching program was a premonition for the change that would unfold.

On June 17th, 2019, I entered my supervisor's office with my agenda and notebook, expecting a typical meeting. What I thought was a routine check-in became the catalyst for one of the most challenging summers of my life—a season that would, in hindsight, lead to a new and welcome chapter.

That's when it hit me: When the universe gives you what you want, don't question how it comes to you. If it's meant to come, it will…and it did.

I found myself leaving my career sooner than expected. But did I really?

In truth, this shift was already part of my vision. Earlier that year, during a vision board workshop, I had placed a picture of myself right in the center, signaling that I was ready to fully embark on my entrepreneurial path and embrace a new way of life. And boy, did I ever.

And I've never looked back. Living in alignment with my core values—freedom, creativity, and relationships—has guided me through this new phase of my life, and I trusted it because I was finally able to fully embrace who I was.

The power of that vision board experience became so clear that has evolved into a regular practice for me and today it's one of my signature workshops. I now deliver these workshops across the globe, helping others design their own visions and dreams. Time and again, I see the value vision boards bring in manifesting desires and setting the direction for what is possible.

It's as if the steps toward this chapter of my life had been unfolding for years, even though I couldn't see it at the time. Those early actions quietly paved the way for what was to come, reminding me that everything was falling into place exactly as it needed to.

Now, looking back on that year, I smile with gratitude and say *thank you.* Despite the discomfort, the uncertainty, and the mistrust, it was all part of the journey. I have come to realize it is not just the hard or unexpected things in life that make us uncomfortable—sometimes, it's the very things we desire.

Admittedly, being in those spaces is challenging. No doubt you know what I am talking about. Why challenging? Because we are dealing with people and, as long as we are dealing with people, we need to understand that their actions and attitudes can significantly impact our own actions and outcomes.

The truth is, I have learned to accept that some folks are just not as self-aware as they should be, often because they are grappling with struggles greater than ours. It is how they navigate their own challenges. As Brené Brown (2015) wisely writes, "I do believe that most of us are really doing the best we can." (*Rising Strong,* p. 107).

This insight was a revelation for me. Viewing others and difficult situations through that lens has been a transformative shift in how I handle challenging circumstances. It lowers my expectations, allowing me to accept what is happening, and it gives me the clarity to decide how best to navigate those situations. I refuse to let anyone, or anything, break me. I choose to protect my peace and embrace happiness—that is the mindset I hold.

Yes, being blindsided was so unsettling, and it took time for me to bounce back. But I recovered. And so will you. We learn, grow, and thrive from every setback. When you've experienced the heartbreak of burying your child, trust me, everything else pales in comparison.

Going through the loss of Danylo and feeling such profound pain has given me a strange kind of assurance: The worst is behind me. I cannot imagine suffering more than I already have. I also believe that both God and Danylo will not allow it to happen. They are my protectors and guides. No matter what life throws my way, I know I will make it through. I will respond in the best way I can—even if, at first, I freeze, like ice cubes freshly out of the freezer, waiting to thaw. Slowly, I will find my calm and respond.

The universe provides exactly what we need, exactly when we need it—it's all about trusting the process. And I do. Every time. How about you?

Patience is a good friend of mine. It is one of my virtues. It has helped me achieve meaningful things in my life. But patience alone isn't enough. It must be accompanied by wisdom, faith, and perseverance—virtues I strongly believe in.

Trusting the process has become my motto, but what a journey it took to get there. Sometimes, the path to where you need to be is anything but smooth. I learned this through an unexpected, unpleasant meeting that caught me completely off guard. It was a hard lesson in understanding that people have their own agendas, and you never know how they will unfold.

I try to believe in the goodness of people, that most want to do right by others. But that's not always the case. Perhaps their definition of what is right has been skewed because of a lack of clarity and interest to solicit information from its source. How often does that happen in life and in the workplace? Deception and mistrust are very real, and navigating those situations can be incredibly difficult. When communication breaks down—or ceases to exist— it's sad to see the lengths some will go to just to prove a point, even when they know it isn't the right way.

I always see the glass as half-full and finding a positive light even in darkness is natural for me. I often wonder: Where does this come from? How did I become this way? And, more importantly, why doesn't everyone think this way?

That is what I struggle with. People will say that I wear rose-coloured glasses despite the darkness. That is true, but what is wrong with that? It has served me pretty well so far, thank you.

The world is made up of all kinds of people. Like animals, people come in all different shapes, sizes, characters, and beings—and that's okay—I get it. It took me a long time to realize that everyone is doing the best with what they have…but are they really?

In today's world, I'm learning not to take anything personally. Let's face it, many people are facing problems, issues, and situations in their personal and professional lives, although it does seem more prevalent than ever. So why would I let their perceptions, attitudes, and demeanours affect me? I have a choice here, and I choose, as much as I can, not to…but that is easier said than done.

We live in such a fast-paced environment. It feels like we are constantly on autopilot, and don't take the time to pause and reflect on our actions, values, and behaviors. Imagine if we all took more time to reflect and introspect—where would we all be? At least better individuals for ourselves, knowing we are wholeheartedly being who we are. And if we're not happy with anything in our lives or about ourselves, remember that we have the power to make those changes. Each of us holds that power. You and me. It is about owning it. Change happens when you decide to change. Change begins with you.

SELF-AWARENESS
UNLOCKED

When we deny the story, it defines us.
When we own the story, we can write a brave new ending.
Brené Brown

Owning who we are begins by first understanding the components that make up who we are. To understand the parts of our lives that make us whole, a concept I often refer to in my workshops is the Wheel of Life, developed by Paul J. Meyer.

Meyer's Wheel of Life comprises seven areas: career, family, financial, intellectual, spiritual, social, and recreational (Meyer, 1960s). I can always tell when something feels off because one of these areas is out of balance. A lack of interest, motivation, or empowerment often indicates that I'm overly focused on one aspect while neglecting others. The Wheel of Life beautifully articulates how I instinctively understood my life—as a pie with various slices.

By placing ourselves at the center of the wheel, we begin to embrace some slices more than others. Depending on where we are in our lives, our focus and energy will shift. For instance, recent graduates often channel their energy into their careers before considering marriage or family but, as they grow and find satisfaction in their careers, their attention may naturally shift toward family and relationships.

We might even juggle multiple areas simultaneously. There is no fixed way to spin this wheel; the key is being aware of how these areas impact our well-being, our values, and our sense of fulfillment.

This awareness helps us recognize when we are off balance, feeling lost, or stuck on autopilot. It serves as a reminder of what we may be neglecting. Deep down, we know where our energy is lacking—intentionally or not. It is up to us to decide when to seek change. Looking at the wheel of life, think about how you are navigating yours. Are there areas where you would like to invest more energy and feel the need to change?

Take a moment to visualize the seven areas of your life—career, family, financial, intellectual, spiritual, social, and recreational—represented as slices of a pie. Draw a circle on a piece of paper and divide it into seven equal sections. Label each section with one of the categories.

Now, rate your current satisfaction in each area on a scale of 1 to 10, where 1 is "not satisfied at all" and 10 is "completely satisfied." Shade in each slice according to your satisfaction level, with 10 being a fully shaded slice and 1 being barely shaded.

Reflection Questions:

- Which areas feel well-balanced, and which ones feel neglected or out of alignment?
- Are there any areas you would like to invest more energy into?
- What small steps can you take today to shift the balance and move closer to your ideal life?

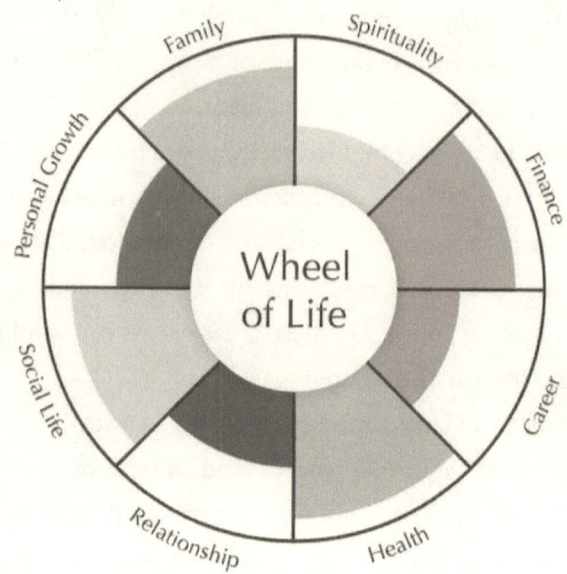

Concept developed by Paul J. Meyer in the 1960s. The wheel represents the balance of key life areas: career, family, financial, intellectual, spiritual, social, and recreational.

Identifying areas of dissatisfaction allows us to determine where to focus our energy and make meaningful changes. We must listen to our inner selves and be honest about what may be missing or where we need to replenish our energy. This wheel helped me recognize when I needed to shift from certain areas to re-engage with myself, giving time and space to the other slices that feed my inner soul. Each area plays a crucial role in our life journey.

I believe we all strive to bring our best selves forward and be true to ourselves. But what does it mean to do so? It begins with understanding who we are and how others perceive us with that same knowledge. You may believe you are a certain way, yet your behavior may convey a different message. Total self-awareness requires the balance of both, and truly is the key to one's success—to your success. Interestingly, according to Tasha Eurich's research many people think they are self-aware, but when measured by the criteria that defines self-awareness, only fifteen percent really are.

As a lifelong learner, my journey of self-discovery has pushed me to continually explore and understand myself in new ways. I once thought I knew a lot about who I was, but not with the depth I do today. In a world where autopilot has become the norm, I, like many others, often forget to pause to reflect on how my actions affect others, or seek feedback to inspire positive change. Recognizing my core values—freedom, creativity, and relationships—was a significant step. It took time to identify and name them, but once I did, I realized that living by these values comes with its own challenges, especially in understanding their impact on those around me.

Self-awareness extends beyond recognizing our values, it also involves understanding our passions, aspirations, and the environments in which we can thrive. It encompasses awareness of our thoughts, behaviors, reactions, and the impact we have on the world. Quite the list, right? As I absorbed Eurich's insights, I became fascinated by narrowing the gap between the science of self-awareness and its practical application in daily life.

I have had the privilege of delivering workshops on topics like 'Reflecting on Yourself in Action' and 'Unveiling the Truth Behind Feedback' to hundreds of people navigating change, transition, and grief. Developing a stronger sense of self and becoming more self-aware is truly a gift that deepens our relationships with loved ones, friends, colleagues, and even ourselves.

The idea of understanding the 'self' more deeply began for me in 2006 when I participated in a leading change initiative training at the university, co-led by Beverley Patwell and Edith Seashore. Triple Impact Coaching opened my eyes to the concept of 'use-of-self' and ignited my passion for learning how we can bring our best selves forward by consciously understanding our patterns and reactions to change, thereby enabling us to navigate it more effectively.

I am grateful to Beverley for creating this deeper desire and passion in me about the 'use-of-self,' and having her as a mentor in my journey ever since has enriched my life in so many ways. Thank you, Beverley!

One tool I learned, which I continue to use and share with my clients, is reframing (Patwell & Seashore, 2006). While it is not a new concept, in triggering moments it a very effective tool to help keep our emotions intact, rather than allowing them to escalate.

For example, imagine you receive critical feedback from a colleague that initially makes you feel defensive and demoralized. Instead of viewing the feedback as a personal attack, you could reframe it as an opportunity for learning and growth. By shifting your perspective, you might think: *This feedback highlights an area where I can improve my skill* or *This is a chance to actually strengthen our working relationship.*

Reframing allows us to approach situations with a growth mindset, transforming potentially negative feelings into motivation and a desire to develop. Yes, easier said than done, but after the initial sting, it is the way to move forward.

An essential part of this reframing process is asking ourselves 'what' questions rather than 'why' questions. 'Why' questions keep us trapped in victim mode—prompting thoughts like *Why did this happen to me?* which do not really serve us. On the other hand, 'what' questions empower us to focus on solutions. For instance, instead of asking, "Why did I receive this feedback?" consider asking, "What can I learn from this feedback?" or "What steps can I take to improve?" This shift not only promotes accountability but also encourages proactive thinking, helping us to move forward with clarity and purpose.

Self-awareness is the meta-skill of all emotional intelligence competencies. It is at the core of understanding ourselves and how we show up in the world. I have been passionate about this topic for years because I believe in the journey—it is a lifelong, continuous process that I embrace each and every day. We gain insight from every experience, good or bad, and we are all capable of making decisions based on those experiences. Ask yourself: How many times have I acted on something I observed, discovered, or experienced, either positively or negatively?

Those 'a-ha' or 'oh no' moments come to us daily. Some can be described as volcanic events that shake us to our core, forcing us to respond to a new reality. Can you recall a time when you were completely caught off guard or were faced with a challenging event? Perhaps it was the death of a loved one, a divorce, or the end of a career. Loss of any kind—sudden or not—shakes us and often leaves us in disbelief. Initially, a flood of questions will arise: How could this be happening? What just happened to me? How will I get past this?

It is normal to ask these questions. but answering them or moving past them is not easy.

When an 'oh no' event occurs, it challenges our personality and forces us to consider how to proceed. Even a planned move can test us. How we handle it—before, during, or after—says a lot about us. Are you action-oriented? A worrier? Do you get stressed easily? Are you adaptable to last-minute changes?

In fact, sometimes everyday life brings discoveries about ourselves, too. The most mundane tasks can offer us quiet moments and space to simply *be*. For instance, washing the dishes has become a meditative experience for me. As I fill the sink with hot, soapy water and slip on my stylish plastic gloves, I feel warmth envelop my hands, creating a soothing sensation. One by one, I wash each item, losing myself in thought and opening up to receive new insights.

Cleaning the dishes has become my excuse—my time—to immerse myself and just *be*…until suddenly, an important thought pops up: Is it significant enough to leave the sink and write it down? Will I forget it? My memory isn't what it used to be…I can't even recall what I just ate! So, off I go to jot it down…the dishes can wait!

Although I would love to believe I can retain everything, my mind just doesn't work that way. So many ideas and thoughts flood in, taking me in different directions. I am guilty of getting overwhelmed, but I am getting better at controlling it by applying the same strategies I share with others, such as learning to quiet my mind from the distractions that come my way, and consciously creating space for clarity.

According to *Psychology Today*, the average person experiences between sixty thousand and eighty thousand thoughts each day—up to four thousand thoughts per hour, or around one thought per second. Think about that! Can you imagine?

Most of these thoughts pass through our minds at lightning speed, some trivial, others with deeper meaning. With so many thoughts constantly swirling, how can we think clearly?

When we obsess over the same thoughts, we become overwhelmed, blocking out the space needed for new ideas and the focus to prioritize what truly matters.

So, how do you create space in your mind for calmness, for new ideas to flow?

Imagine driving down a dark road, not knowing where you're headed. The hum of the engine is the only constant sound, but in the back seat the kids are giggling and talking over each other, creating a blur of voices. The dog is barking frantically, and you're struggling to read the GPS screen in the dim light. Your phone rings—it's your significant other—and now you're juggling multiple things, each pulling your attention in a different direction.

That is how our minds often feel—like a jumble of noise and distraction, each thought demanding our attention, making it almost impossible to focus. Can you relate?

The chaos swirling in our minds is exactly what hinders our ability to stay focused, preventing new ideas and thoughts from taking root. Our brains crave quiet, a moment of stillness amidst the frenzy. Finding space for this peace is absolutely critical for our well-being. Trust me, I cannot stress this enough.

One practice that helps me achieve some mental clarity is a daily brain-dump. It's like hitting a reset button for my thoughts. I take a notebook, date a page, and start writing down everything that's swirling around in my head—no judgment, no stopping, just letting the words flow until I've emptied my mind. I usually do this for about three to four minutes, and by the end, I already feel my mind lightening, clearing, and calming.

Once I've emptied out my thoughts, I take a moment to read what I've written. I begin to notice patterns or recurring themes—those thoughts that are occupying valuable space in my mind. This helps me understand what I need to focus on. Some thoughts demand immediate action, others are ideas for future projects, and sometimes it is simply a reminder to breathe, go for a walk, or write more.

Another method I use to release my thoughts is to speak them aloud—often when I'm alone, in the comfort of solitude. Just hearing my voice articulate the clutter in my head brings a sense of relief. It is the act of releasing, whether through writing or speaking, that matters. That release is what allows us to reclaim our mental space and, in turn, create room for new, clearer, and more purposeful thoughts.

When you need to have that difficult conversation, or find yourself angry about something or someone, rehearse it with yourself. Say aloud what you feel. The beauty of this is that the other person doesn't hear it, but you get to release your feelings. By doing this, you'll feel lighter and be better prepared for the real conversation when the time comes. Try it next time. Trust me, it works.

It is all about how we choose to react. And yes, we do have that choice—just like every other choice in our lives. Freedom is a choice. Drinking from a glass, whether it's half-full or half-empty, is a choice. It is about deciding how you see the glass and what you'll do with it. Struggles and challenges are real, and we often find ourselves asking, "Why me?" But asking "Why?" won't change the situation. Instead of going down a rabbit hole of self-pity, we need to be mindful of our thoughts and self-talk. Mindset is everything.

So, instead of asking, "Why did this happen?" or "Why don't I like this person?" ask a 'what' question. For example, "What can I learn from this?" or "What is it about this person that's making me feel this way?"

Shifting to a 'what' question will make all the difference. Of course, building this mindset takes time—it's easier to stay in a place of sorrow and victimhood because it validates our feelings. But staying there doesn't solve anything. Growth is hard. Nothing worth striving for is easy—whether it's learning more, being more, or improving for your own benefit, not for anyone else.

I often find myself pondering why the desire to learn and expand our horizons comes more naturally to some people than to others. Is it simply a matter of how we are wired and how our minds operate?

Recently, after watching Emilie Wapnick's TED Talk, I stumbled upon the term 'multipotentiality.' This discovery sparked an 'a-ha' moment for me: I don't need to fit into a box. I can be good at and interested in many things, each bringing out the best in me and aligning with who I am.

As Wapnick explores in her talk, embracing this variety can lead to a more fulfilling and authentic life. (Ted.com)

I have also learned that it is perfectly okay not to follow a linear path. Many people struggle to decide what career they want to pursue, often feeling lost along the way. Regardless of the path you choose, what truly matters is that you pursue what makes you happy and remain steadfast in your journey. Are you clear on the path you wish to take?

My clarity emerged through trial and error. In 1986, after graduating from a private secretarial college in Montreal, The Motherhouse, I explored various industries in the private sector but soon realized that higher education resonated with me far more.

Throughout my twenty-five-plus years at the university, the common thread was my passion for helping others—a passion that shone through in all the roles I held related to learning and development. It was my lifelong strength. Although I spent many years with the one institution, I actively sought out positions that offered opportunities for growth, thereby always satisfying my inner need for challenge and development.

I have come to understand myself well: when I feel bored or stagnant, I need change. At one point, I wondered if something was wrong with me for feeling that way. How could others stay in the same position for twenty or thirty years?

I didn't understand then, but I do now. Their journey is their own, and mine is mine. For me, growth is a natural part of who I am, and when I evolve, my work must evolve with me. Not everyone needs that level of change, but I did—I do.

While pursuing my coaching certification in 2016, I created a personal credo that keeps me aligned with my true self. It has become a guiding tool, helping me navigate my career and life wholeheartedly by simply being me. It has grounded me, kept me focused, and allowed me to move forward authentically.

Before I share mine with you, I invite you to think about your own personal credo. What principles guide you? What values shape your decisions and keep you aligned with your true self? Take a moment to reflect on this as you craft your own personal credo.

- Reflect on core values: What are the most important values in your life? These could be related to love, integrity, health, family, growth, or anything that feels essential to who you are.
- Write down your principles: What are the principles or actions that help you live by your core values? Think about the daily practices, habits, or mindsets that keep you grounded and authentic.
- Create your credo: Craft a statement or a set of guiding principles that reflect how you want to live and what you believe will keep you aligned with your best self. This can be a few sentences or a list, just like mine below.

Once you have written your credo, keep it somewhere visible, or refer to it when you need a reminder to stay true to yourself.

Now that you have had a chance to reflect on your credo, here is mine. These ten statements keep me aligned with my true self and guide me as I navigate life.

To foster a happy and healthy life through personal choice and being fully true to myself:

1. *Commit to doing something and stick to it* (if you move toward something, it will move toward you).
2. *Manage my stress more effectively* (counteract the stress with yoga, breathing breaks, mini-meditations throughout the day, exercise, play, positive self-talk).
3. *Take appropriate time to rest and get enough good sleep* (six hours isn't cutting it—aiming for at least eight).
4. *Respect my own boundaries...people will respect me more* (practice by saying 'no'). Yes!
5. *Be true to myself* (check in with myself about who I really am, despite my circumstances and outside influences. What do I really love? What do I long to do? How would I love to live? Shift my life toward living more authentically).
6. *Be childlike* (cultivate the very best of the child within me. Practice childlike awe for majestic things, childlike silliness, childlike hope, and childlike play. Recapture the little girl in me).
7. *Don't wait* (do not put off life—don't wait until things are perfect. Figure out how I can start now and start small). This is a hard one for me, but not when it comes to travel.
8. *Give my heart priority over my head* (practical, logical me). Start the plan in my heart first—what would I love to experience? Then, use my head to figure out how I might get there. The heart's much kinder and more optimistic.
9. *Have faith* (believe that there is something greater helping me out in life). I know it. There are endless studies that show the benefits of faith and spiritual practice on physical health, mental health, and happiness.
10. *When my body says stop, listen to it.*

Let me repeat this one:

When my body says stop, listen to it.

How often do you listen to your body?

Recently, this has been quite an eye-opener for me. Safeguarding our bodies requires establishing good, mindful self-care practices. Sure, you read about it and you consciously, and subconsciously, know about it, but is it an easy practice for you to follow?

It was Friday morning when my phone rang, waking me up. On the other end, my dearest friend spoke in a low, trembling voice, her pain evident in every word. Her illness was terminal. A week earlier, she had called me similarly, and I had jumped into action. That morning, my physiotherapy appointment had been cancelled, so I quickly pulled myself together, ran to the store to get what she needed, and then spent the morning by her side.

This time, though, something was different. Her words reached me, but my body didn't react. I stayed in bed, feeling unshakable exhaustion. It wasn't indifference, it was depletion. I'd had a long week and I knew I was running on empty.

My day was already planned—in the morning I was scheduled for a much-needed self-care routine at a wellness centre, and the afternoon was set aside to spend with my ill friend. I stuck to my plan.

When I shared this with my boyfriend during our morning call, he commended me. "Good for you," he said, "You are honoring yourself and still showing up for her."

For once, I didn't feel guilty.
For once, I didn't abandon myself.

I honored my personal growth routine at a time when I was feeling particularly stressed and overstretched. I listened to my body, knowing I couldn't pour from an empty cup. That decision—to put my needs first for a few hours—wasn't selfish, it was essential.

We must give to ourselves before we can give to others. We must keep our bodies healthy and resilient. When we listen to our bodies, we're not just safeguarding our well-being; we're strengthening our ability to be present for the people who need us most.

That day, I began with my morning self-care:

- Stretching as I woke up, thanking God with a smile for another day.
- Meditating for 10-15 minutes while soothing my dry eyes with a compress.
- Sitting by the window with natural light, selecting an angel card, journaling my gratitude, and setting intentions for the day.
- Brain-dumping for 5-10 minutes to clear mental clutter.
- Moving my body, either with a 15-minute fitness routine or a nature walk…ideally, both!

When I left the wellness center, I felt renewed, calm, and fully present. My body was settled. I listened to it and said, "Yes," to myself.

Later that afternoon, I fulfilled my promise to my dearest friend, Terry. I sat by her side, talked with her, cared for her, and gave her my full attention and presence—all in good spirits.

Terry passed away on March 19, 2025—one of our "four musketeers" gone. What? It is so hard to believe, even though I was preparing for this day.

She always said, "You know Barbie, I won't live long; I'll be the first to go." She called it and she prepared us. She knew. Even so, it still didn't feel real to get that text message from her beautiful daughter at 5:30 that afternoon. It was just thirty minutes before I had to present the final class of the course I was teaching., I paused. *No. She can't be gone.*

I made my way to the faculty lounge to call her daughter, Bella. We cried, we talked, and then I regrouped for what awaited me—thirty excited students, guest panelists, and a celebratory potluck to end the night. The show must go on, as they say. I didn't let up, except with the other musketeers, Tina and Enza, who happened to be on my panel. We all had our moments—together and separately. That is how it is when you grieve. We each need to find the way that works for us.

We regrouped. The class began. It was engaging, rich, and full of laughter and accolades. That's what Terry would have wanted. "Don't cry for me," she would say. "I am healed. I am in a better place. And I will serve you and guide you from above." And so, she will.

On the day of her memorial service, pictures taken thirteen years earlier of her and Enza's milestone birthday celebration in New York City appeared on my newsfeed. What a time to treasure, and a sign from her! We will always be the four musketeers! I will not only hold onto the twenty-five years of shared laughter, friendship, hardship, and love, but also to the gift of those final moments knowing they were among our last.

Throughout her illness, I visited Terry whenever I could, cherishing every moment and managing to raise a smile or laugh as we planned our next girl getaway. I even brought my manuscript to the hospital and read what I had written about our friendship. I will never forget the joy on her face as she listened, her smile radiating with warmth. That moment of pure connection will stay with me forever. I gave her what she needed as she was preparing to leave this world.

Throughout her illness, Terry was my cheerleader. She believed she would be at my book signing and celebrating my sixtieth birthday with me—even if we couldn't travel far. I held onto that hope with her, right to her final days. Now, as I enter the final stages of my book writing, I know that Terry is celebrating with me, watching from above. I can almost hear her voice, clear as day, saying, "Congrats, Chomyk! You did it! I knew you would, and I am so proud of you!"

Her presence, her spirit, is with me. I feel her pride and love surrounding me as I approach this sacred milestone. Just today, I returned from a much-needed walk—one of those walks where your body moves, but your soul leads. My instinct was to dial her number, just as I always did, to chat before she began supper for her student. But this time, I looked up to the sky and spoke out loud, "Terry, I'm coming to the end. I'm nervous. I'm scared. But I feel you with me."

I thanked her—for her strength, her faith in me, her unwavering love. And I remembered something Oprah once said, a truth that struck me deeply: When our loved ones pass on, we often feel their presence even more powerfully. Their spirits are no longer confined to form—they become a part of us, woven into our being.

That is how I feel about her now. Not gone, but transformed. She has become another angel walking with me, guiding me. And knowing Terry, she won't do it quietly. She was never one to go unnoticed. I can almost hear her voice, vibrant and full of life, cheering me on from the heavens. That thought—her laugh, her fierce love—brings a smile through the tears.

She is still here. Just in her own unforgettable way.

And what makes it even more special is that Terry shares a birthday with my second son, Adrian—a sign, I believe, that she will always be woven into the fabric of my life. She was there from the very beginning, from the moment Adrian was conceived in Mexico, the very place where our lifelong friendship took root. Though she may no longer be here in the physical sense, I feel her presence in the quiet whispers of encouragement, in the warmth that floods my heart when I recall our memories, and in the unshakable knowing that true love never leaves us—it simply transforms.

In those sacred moments when I need her most, it is as though she finds a way to reach me, to guide me, to remind me that her spirit still dances through my life. So, I listen—closely. To my heart. To my body. And to the gentle, unmistakable signs that she is still here, loving me in her own timeless way.

And that is why establishing a self-care routine is not only crucial during times of stress and trauma, but also an essential way to live. Honoring our needs and listening to our bodies creates the foundation for showing up as our best selves—not just in our personal lives, but also in how we navigate our careers and unique journeys.

Terry always used to say, "Tania, you work too hard, take time off for you." She always knew how to have fun, even when she worked hard herself. We shared an entrepreneurial spirit, even if we were on completely different paths and missions. Honoring myself was important, even when I struggled to do so. I often pushed forward, driven by ambition and purpose, yet she reminded me that rest and joy were just as essential as hard work.

My commitment to self-care has been essential not just for my personal well-being, but also for how I navigate my career. As someone with many interests and passions, I have learned that honoring my needs—physically, emotionally, and creatively—is key to thriving in my ever-evolving journey.

It was through this lens that I came to embrace my identity as a multipotentialite, a term Emily Wapnick so aptly describes. Just as I need to balance ambition with rest, I also had to learn to balance my many interests and passions in a way that honors both my drive and my well-being.

Whether you have multiple interests or not, whether you follow a traditional career path or forge your own, every individual must navigate their career and life in their unique way. Thank you, Emily Wapnick, for emphasizing that there is a place for multipotentialites like me—and so many others.

Being a multipotentialite illuminates both who I am and the challenges I face daily. My mind loves the diversity of interests and creative ideas. My energy thrives on it, but managing multiple pursuits can also be quite exhausting. Focus can be particularly challenging for us multipotentialites, and procrastination often becomes our best friend. When the urge to fulfill a meaningful goal or embark on a new path intensifies, the decision seems easier to make. Those moments energize me and give me a sense of purpose. When I need to act, I do. I excel under pressure, experiencing bursts of energy followed by a profound sense of release. However, this cycle can leave me feeling emotionally drained, prompting a need to disengage and reconnect with myself. It is a cycle I am fully aware of.

Can you relate? Some decisions I've made in the past—like selling our home just three weeks after Danylo's passing or resigning from a job that bored me—were made in haste. Yet, these choices opened space for movement and progress, introducing the newness I craved.

Reflecting on this, I see procrastination and patience as intertwined forces that allowed me to grieve in my own way. There is no defined timeline in the grieving process, so I tapped into what worked for me at that time. When I needed to move forward, I did so at my own pace, irrespective of my circumstances. Procrastination served its purpose, helping me avoid situations that could create discomfort. While some may view this as stalling my healing, I see it as a deliberate strategy that allowed me to move forward more effectively. It granted me the opportunity to continue cautiously on my journey, filled with trust and patience.

So, rather than perceiving procrastination as a negative, I invite you to consider that it could be a blessing—an opportunity to embrace what you truly need at the right time—and how you can leverage it to bring out the very best in yourself.

When I reflect on the idea of being traditional versus non-traditional, I have mixed feelings. There is a part of me that once dreamed of the perfect family, a successful career, and a happy life—dreams that, in many ways, I did achieve. Yet, when I look back at my educational and career journey, I see how far I veered from the traditional path. Earning a Bachelor in Vocational Education with a focus on Business/English was no small feat, especially while working full-time.

However, despite this achievement, I never fully embraced a traditional teaching role, except for the required teacher training and when my career at the university recently came full circle. The typical classroom environment, with its emphasis on planning and evaluation, never quite captured my interest. Instead, I was drawn to applying my teaching skills in a more hands-on way—through my roles at the university in human resources and employee training and development. Those roles weren't about following a prescribed process, rather they were about empowering people with the skills they needed to succeed. That focus on people, rather than process, has always been at the core of my work—then and now. Designing and creating my own materials, based on the knowledge I have acquired, is how I share my expertise with others.

I did explore several outside contract jobs, including teaching business English to technical and sales professionals, and offering business courses…

all while working full-time. My goal was to stretch my skills, put my learning into practice, and continue growing along the way. Higher education played a key role in my career by offering opportunities to do just that. But inevitably, I would hit roadblocks, lose interest, and feel the urge to shift again. That's when my multipotentialite tendencies would resurface, signaling it was time for change. I was never afraid to dive into something new—whether it was pursuing a new desire, setting a fresh goal, or uncovering a hidden talent.

EXPLORING NEW HORIZONS

Do not go where the path may lead,
go instead where there is no path and leave a trail.
Ralph Waldo Emerson

In November 2022, I took to the stage in a very different capacity—or at least somewhat different. I delivered an inspirational speech in front of a live audience at one of the most beautiful centres in Toronto, Ontario, Canada. My speech, *The Journey*, was written alongside my coach, Rina, and focused on the theme of *Evolution*. It is a legacy piece that honored three generations of Ukrainian women in my family, their quest for freedom, and what that journey means for me today. Talk about a stretch from what I had been doing.

It all started with my latest vision: to inspire people by sharing my story, to make a greater impact in the world and to help others overcome loss and failure, not just to survive, but to thrive. To earn my place on that stage, I had to be a finalist—one of the top ten. I made it there in June 2022 with my first speech, *The Million-Dollar Family*, which focused on the theme of *Healing*. That story had been waiting to come out for years. In fact, I wrote that five-minute speech from the research paper I had written during my master's degree, *Life...after the loss of a child.*

Similar to how I'm writing this book, I took a focused approach, carving out dedicated writing time, letting the words flow. Professor Bernardelli had created a space for me to grieve, to write, to express my emotions. And now, twenty-two years later, I write this book with the intention of helping as many people as I can—not just to cope with their grief but to see that even amid the darkest clouds, there is light and love waiting to be found.

When I first entered Speaker Slam, I so wasn't in it for the competition. I simply wanted to learn how to write an inspirational speech and deliver the story of my son, Danylo. I needed his name to be remembered, to be heard, to never be forgotten—for him, and for me.

The first theme for 2022 was *Catalyst*, and after countless rehearsals, I found myself in a critical moment. It was the night before the submission deadline. I had rehearsed with Larissa, and I'd spent hours practicing in front of the camera, but as the clock ticked down, I became paralyzed.

I called my boyfriend, Ken, and said, "I'm not sending it in." He asked, "Why? You worked so hard!" But something in me wasn't ready. I couldn't explain it, but I knew it wasn't the right time.

I told my coach, Rina, that I was stepping away. She replied, "Tania, it's a process. It's all part of your journey." And she was right. Three months later, a new theme emerged—*Healing*—and I knew that's where my son's story belonged.

I entered the speech competition again, this time with a deeper connection to the message. I made it into the top ten and, shockingly, a week later, in front of four judges and a virtual crowd, I placed third in my first-ever speaking competition! Wow!

On November 18, 2022, the weekend after the twenty-fourth anniversary of Danylo's death, I stood proudly wearing my mother's hand-embroidered Ukrainian blouse and a long black skirt. Barefoot, I walked on stage and began delivering one of the most powerful, emotional speeches of my life. *The Journey* took the audience through three generations of pain and joy, strength and resilience, demonstrating how struggle is an essential part of evolution. My message was to never give up on hope.

Though I didn't place first, second, or third, I was proud. I came in fifth place out of twelve speakers. At first, I felt a bit disappointed—I had hoped for top three—but there was something deep inside of me that knew I wasn't ready for the win. At times during my delivery, I felt frozen in place, speaking more like I was reciting a monologue than delivering a speech. *If only I had moved a little more.* Some may have seen it as perfect, others may not have, especially after witnessing some more flamboyant performances. But I got through it, and despite a few moments of doubt, I felt the energy of my guides and supporters lifting me up.

They created a legacy video of my speech, and when I watch it now, I am struck by how powerful it is—heartbreaking yet empowering. It is a reflection of how far I've come in my own journey, and a tribute to those who are still fighting their own battles, particularly those in Ukraine today. This speech, and the footage, extends far beyond my family's story—it's a story shared by so many others who are living through war and tragedy.

I never thought it would have such an impact. It was beyond what I could have imagined. My mother, watching from the audience, was beaming with pride. She cried the whole time. Maybe she was reliving her own life through me, or maybe we were both reliving it together. Her struggles were part of my journey, and now they are part of my daughter's. The story continues, each generation carrying forward the weight and the lessons of the past.

This journey reminds me that history often repeats itself. Patterns will keep repeating unless we make conscious choices to change them. Yes, the environment we live in influences some of our decisions but, ultimately, we are the ones who choose: Will we work? Will we study? Will we choose happiness?

I feel blessed to live in a country that is free from war, where I feel protected and safe. But deep down, I always knew that fear wouldn't serve me. Despite moments of fear throughout my life, I never let it take over. I always felt that I was protected and guided by angels who walked beside me.

One day when I was about eight years old, while walking home from school, something unsettling happened. I always took the same route home for lunch—a time I loved because it meant watching *The Flintstones* and savoring one of Tato's culinary creations. That day, as I walked, smiling and lost in my usual daydreams, I suddenly noticed a man approaching. He was wearing a raincoat and, as he came closer, I realized with a shock that his coat was open and he was exposing himself.

I froze for a moment, unsure of what to do, but then instinct took over and I ran away as fast as I could. I glanced back once or twice, but he was gone almost as quickly as he had appeared. For a while I avoided that street but, eventually, I returned. Somehow, I let it pass—it was just a fleeting moment. The fear faded too, shifting from just "forget everything and run" to how I embrace things today with "face everything and rise."

Looking back now, I realize that this ability to move forward, to create an invisible shield, wasn't random. The resilience that shaped me wasn't mine alone—it was built from the strength of my ancestors. Those who came before me had endured their own traumas and struggles, yet they found ways to survive and thrive. Their legacy of strength has been a source of power, keeping me steady in moments of fear while fueling a deep belief that I can rise above anything. It is their strength that has taught me to survive, to hope, and to keep going.

When Tato had a little too much to drink and wasn't allowed back into the house, he would try to get my sister or me to let him in. My sister would be anxious and afraid, but I'd always say, "*It's okay. It'll be fine.*" *I felt an unwavering confidence that Daddy would never hurt us—he loved us too much. Maybe it was naïve, but it was true—he never did. We were his pride and joy. He was struggling, engaged in his own battles that he didn't know how to face, and I didn't want him to suffer alone.*

Every day after school or work, I would ride my bicycle to his place and make sure he was okay. Over time, he began visiting us again, joining us for dinner when Mom came home from work, tending to the garden like old times. It was as if he'd never really left, though he'd still go back to his apartment when it got dark. We all adjusted to this new rhythm—seeing them together in peace brought me comfort, even if it meant watching him leave every night. It was enough for me that they could find a way to coexist and share our lives in harmony.

Even with his struggles, at first Tato couldn't stand being completely apart from us. But slowly, he came to accept the arrangement which seemed to lessen his anxiety and bring him a measure of peace.

Still, if only he'd been living with us in 1990—on May 26—that day would have started very differently.

May 26, 1990—the day I got married.

Tato missed that day, but not because he didn't want to be there.

When he saw my wedding album for the first time, tears rolled down his face and the pain of that moment gripped me deeply because there was more to that day than I had ever told anyone…although the *truth did eventually find its way out over a glass of wine and a daring question one summer night.*

My biggest supporter, my father who cherished me, missed the happiest day of my life. I still carry a bit of sorrow from that, but I've learned to forgive myself—and, in a way, to forgive my mother, too. In the end, Tato loved us fiercely and perhaps he knew that, even with the gaps and imperfections, he would always be part of our family's journey.

This episode in my life has been a hard one to face. Only recently, while preparing for my writing retreat and reflecting on the people I needed to forgive, did I realize how deeply I had to forgive myself too.

Forgiveness, I've come to see, is more about finding peace within ourselves than excusing others. It is letting go of what was, releasing what has passed, and choosing to move forward with it. There is no changing the past, but it has taught me the value of being fully present and cherishing what truly matters—our relationships with ourselves and with others. These are the memories we carry forward. I've come to understand that everyone, including myself, does the best they can with what they know, and have, at any given time.

Today, my mother is the only one left from her family, and I often find myself torn between impatience and compassion as she repeats her stories. But then, I pause, take a breath, and remind myself: Tania, this is who she is now, and these stories are part of her legacy. Sharing them is her way of ensuring she's remembered, and I honor that need. I know that one day, she will no longer be here to tell them, and I will miss her dearly. In fact, I can hardly imagine life without her, even though I am fully aware that she is ninety-one years old. She has always been and will always be my strongest advocate, my teacher, my biggest supporter—my precious, dearest mother.

In moments when I see myself in her, I wonder to myself: *How can I evolve from her strengths to be my best self?*

I know that my positivity can sometimes overwhelm others, especially those who don't share it. Confronting my mother on certain things isn't easy, for either of us. She withdraws, and I am left feeling the sting of that resistance. But now, I realize there's no need to change her. My purpose is to be there for her, to listen, support, and create little joys—like our regular Sunday brunches or shopping outings. Ken often reminds me, "Leopards don't change their spots," and in some ways, they even become more defined. I take what I can, and when I need to step back, I know how to pause, recharge, and then re-engage.

Our routines—our morning hello, our evening goodnight—bring us both comfort. When one of us misses a call, the other always reaches out, and I'm usually the one calling first. Funny how the expectation has always been that we call her. Now, few people reach out to her; many of her friends and family are gone. Growing old is lonely, especially as that familiar circle shrinks. Yet she stays active, finding meaning in her church and community, looking forward to our Sunday brunches. We all need something to look forward to, and as she often tells me, "Wait, Tania, until you reach my age." I can only respond, "If only I'll be so blessed." To live to ninety-one—what a testament to resilience.

That generation—the survivors of war, scarcity, and hardship—have somehow endured, and their approach to life and family is so grounded. Meanwhile, because our lives are stretched in so many directions, full of responsibilities and stresses, we often don't stop to savor what is right in front of us. If we keep pushing forward without pause, we will eventually burn out. We have to remember that stress is more than an inconvenience—it is a quiet thief of well-being. Though it's rarely cited as a direct cause, stress sets off ripples within us that, if left unattended, can undermine our health, spirit, and joy in living.

NURTURING THE SELF

*You yourself, as much as anybody in the entire universe,
deserve your love and affection.*
Buddha

Keeping stress bottled up inside is never the answer, yet so many of us do it... until it's too late. We are all born with cancer cells, but why are they triggered in one person and not another? Genetics can certainly play a role, with family history predisposing some more than others, but what about the rest? Are they living under the weight of constant stress, believing they can simply endure it; or are they silently carrying on without recognizing the toll it's taking?

Research underscores the profound impact of chronic stress on our longevity. A study by the Finnish Institute for Health and Welfare found that heavy stress can reduce life expectancy by approximately 2.8 years for men and 2.3 years for women. For some reason, I feel it reduces it even more.

These findings have compelled me to make intentional choices that reduce stress and invite peace into my life. Prioritizing well-being isn't just about living well—it's about living longer. While I cannot always control what enters my life, I can control what I choose to carry with me.

I've learned that self-care is the most effective preventative measure against stress and is absolutely crucial for our well-being. I didn't truly understand the value of self-care until later in life. Perhaps it's because I was already taking care of myself—looking after my inner peace and space—but there came a point when I realized that, if I couldn't protect my own well-being or if I felt tremendous stress, my intuition would shout, "You need to get out of here, Tania!"

And how did I know?

My body told me.

My mind would race, my jaw would clench, my face and body felt numb, and I didn't know where to start or what to do next. The only thing that I could do was breathe. I realized over time that self-care is how I learned to settle my body, increase my ability to manage life's stress, and create more room for my nervous system to find a sense of coherence and flow. Healing is a practice. As Resmaa Menakem (2017) emphasizes in *My Grandmother's Hands*, few skills are more essential than the ability to settle our bodies. When we can do this, we are more likely to be calm, alert, and fully present, no matter what is happening around us.

Safeguarding our body requires establishing mindful, consistent self-care practices.

For me, the first step to self-care was quieting the noise—the external and internal clutter—so that I could actually listen and feel. Growing up, we never really talked about our emotions. There was no space to validate what I was feeling. If I expressed myself, I risked hurting someone's feelings, but when I stayed silent, nothing was addressed.

I remember when I was little, one of the highest priests from our community came to bless our home. As was customary, we weren't allowed to wear shoes inside, so when I rushed to the door to greet him, I couldn't help but notice his feet. Without thinking, I blurted out in Ukrainian, "God, you can't come into our house with your shoes on—we are not allowed to. We *all* have to take our shoes off."

My mother's face turned crimson with embarrassment, but the priest—who resembled a figure of authority to me with his long black cloak, flowing gray beard, and soft, calming voice—gently lifted me up with a big smile and said, "God bless you, child, for being so honest." And he slowly took off his big black shoes. In that moment, my directness was not only accepted, it was also embraced. My innocence and honesty were not judged, instead met with warmth and kindness.

I was a child who spoke my mind. I had a particular fascination with purses and would often approach women sitting in the auditorium, asking them to show me what was inside. I even once commented to a dear lady who wore a lot of makeup, "Hmm, my mother doesn't have that much makeup on her face." My words came out effortlessly, completely genuine, and without any malice.

Today, though, telling the truth doesn't always come so easily. People don't always want to hear it, especially when it's unsolicited. Now, I find myself thinking twice before I speak, waiting for someone to ask for my thoughts, and trying to navigate the fine line of political correctness to avoid offending anyone. It seems that as we grow, the simple honesty of childhood becomes tangled with the expectations of what others want to hear.

It seems that these days, almost everyone can be offended by the smallest comment—even our own family members. I know that when something is said that doesn't land well, it often speaks more about the receiver than the messenger. Still, that doesn't stop me from feeling the pull to be honest—just with a bit more awareness. Unsolicited feedback is rarely welcomed, but I believe feedback is essential for self-awareness. After all, if we think we come across one way, but others perceive us differently, shouldn't we be made aware of that? Blind spots, which we all have, only become visible when we open ourselves to feedback.

I've worked to turn these 'blind spots' into part of my open area, as described in the Johari Window model (Luft & Ingham, 1955). The Johari Window helps us understand self-awareness and interpersonal relationships. It divides our awareness into four quadrants: the open area—things known by both ourselves and others; the blind spot—things others know about us that we don't; the hidden area—things we know about ourselves but keep hidden; and the unknown area—things neither we nor others are aware of.

I now know that when I'm tuning out, it is evident in my demeanor and gaze. Similarly, when I am hyper-focused, I know I can come across as standoffish or aloof.

This leads me to a deeper lesson I have learned through personal hardship—the grief that followed my profound loss. In those early days, grief could have consumed me. There were times it felt like it would, but I knew I had to find a way to manage it, so it wouldn't take over my life any more than it needed to. I had a family to care for, and they needed me as much as I needed to move forward. Grief, like stress, demands attention, but it also requires resilience—the kind of resilience that doesn't deny pain, but learns to coexist with it.

My resilience allowed me to face grief without letting it control my every moment. It was not about "getting over it," but about learning to live with it in a way that didn't diminish my energy nor my capacity for joy.

Choosing resilience—choosing to move forward while honoring my grief—has been a cornerstone of my journey toward self-care. I had to trust that, just like with stress, the key to not letting grief overwhelm me lay in the choices I made. How I took care of myself, how I allowed myself moments of rest and peace, and how I consciously sought joy in the smallest things—all of these contributed to my well-being and helped me manage my emotions.

Resilience doesn't mean you don't feel the weight of loss; it means you give yourself permission to live, despite it.

FREEDOM BEYOND
BOUNDARIES

Success is not the key to happiness. Happiness is the key to success.
Albert Schweitzer

Stepping off the career ladder sooner than I had anticipated felt like a double-edged sword—a tremendous weight on my shoulders, but also a profound sense of relief.

It was as if I finally had permission to embrace who I was, with all my other interests and ambitions. Throughout my career, I'd always brought an entrepreneurial spirit to my work, whether teaching on the side, coaching clients, or selling products. Realizing I could do both—and more—was liberating, especially as my motivation waned in the nine to five, day-to-day administrative routine. I wasn't using my talents and skills in ways that fulfilled me, and I knew something had to change.

That shift came one hot summer day during a big swim meet competition in 2018. While browsing the vendor stands, I met a woman selling SweetLegs, the most comfortable leggings I'd ever felt. These 'kitteny-soft' leggings didn't just feel amazing, they were a magnet for anyone's touch. I instantly fell in love and bought a matching pair for my daughter and me. I also invited her to my home to host a SweetLegs party.

That fall, I welcomed friends and co-workers into my home for a SweetLegs

119

party that was a hit. So much so, in fact, that I was encouraged to become an independent representative for the company.

Selling SweetLegs opened doors I hadn't expected. I connected with women who, while interested in leggings, shared much more of themselves than just their style preferences. And when the pandemic struck, leggings became a go-to staple of many wardrobes. Everyone wanted comfort at home, and SweetLegs delivered—soft, stretchy, and flattering for every shape and size. I loved seeing women of all sizes feel confident, and I realized how much joy I found in helping people feel good about themselves. Self-confidence, after all, is the best outfit.

My SweetLegs business took off and, as I re-organized my home space, clients would come over and often leave with more than just leggings. It was a great chapter in my career. Other opportunities started to emerge for me— perhaps it was because I wanted more than just to sell a product, I wanted to create meaningful connections and lasting impacts for my clients.

Knowing I wanted to support women in deeper, more meaningful ways, I realized that taking on more coaching clients was the next step. After developing my workshop on self-reflection in action, I began guiding clients on their own journeys of self-discovery. Interestingly, I didn't fully grasp that while I was taking them on this journey, I was continuing my own.

As it turned out, I was organically creating a course without even realizing it. Over time, I packaged the insights and skills I'd gathered into a program, which I eventually delivered to the West Island Women's Centre in the Spring of 2023.

At first, when approached to deliver the course, I hesitated. But as the weeks unfolded, I saw the pieces coming together in a way that felt almost effortless. The course was a huge success, and they wanted more.

From there, wonderful things began happening. I was honored to be recognized as one of the top fifteen coaches in Montreal—for two years in a row! This recognition validated my work and encouraged me to push further. When a participant shared a testimonial about the impact I'd had on her life, I was in awe. That feedback reminded me that I truly had the ability to help women take ownership of their lives and to guide them in unveiling their passionate core through journeys of self-discovery.

People often tell me that I live my truth and that I practice what I preach. And I do—it feels incredible. But I've been stuck plenty of times too, caught in moments when I felt I wasn't living my purpose or truth. It's during those times that I have had to make a conscious choice to reconnect with the real me.

Imposter syndrome and moments of isolation do creep in, especially as a solopreneur. To counter them, I meditate, surround myself with joyful reminders, and focus on gratitude. I reach out to my loving critics, knowing that I am not alone. That support keeps me grounded.

The pandemic has transformed the landscape of workplaces. Many people have pivoted towards work that resonates with their values, no longer willing to extend themselves for organizations that don't align with their core beliefs.

Alignment is essential. Solopreneur ship has become more common, as has the concept of a portfolio career—a mix of contracts, income streams, and varied work that lets people exercise their power of choice. Now, individuals can leverage their skills and talents across a broader spectrum, making a more significant impact while creating lives that balance work and personal fulfillment.

In today's climate, work-life *balance* feels outdated. It is more about work-life *integration*. This isn't about blending or blurring boundaries, it's about integrating work and life with your whole self. You show up as the same person in both contexts and embrace authenticity wholeheartedly.

That is how my life feels now. I bring my true self to every part of my life—there's no need to cover or mask any part of who I am. Professionalism remains, of course—I know when to speak up and when not to.

I remember sharing this with Ken on our first date. He looked at me, intrigued, and asked, "What do you mean you know your place?"

I explained that it's about timing and tone—choosing the right words when I need to convey a message but knowing when it's better to stay silent. Perhaps it is the way I was raised, or just the maturity that comes with age.

I am still direct, when necessary, but I strive to convey my messages in ways that don't feel confrontational.

Ken once called me a 'cerebral assassin.' At first, I wasn't sure whether to take it as a compliment or an acknowledgment that I have a knack for subtly getting my way. But when I really think about it, maybe that's my feminine power at work. Why not use a more thoughtful, strategic approach to get what I want—one that respects both myself and others?

To me, that's the most effective way to navigate life. It is not about manipulation; it's about tapping into a quieter, more intentional strength. Still, I often question: Is there a deeper need beneath this? Is it simply about always getting what I want? Or is it a reflection of a more nuanced need to communicate and act with purpose and authenticity?

Regardless of the deeper questions, I have decided to embrace my approach. It works for me, and I will continue to honor it.

One thing I know for sure is that I'm always learning. I once thought that as a mother, my role was to teach my children the lessons I had learned but the truth is, I learn just as much from them as they do from me. Larissa and Adrian have been my anchors, showing me aspects of myself I had not fully recognized.

I'll never forget the time Adrian said, "Mom, you know you're not a great listener."

Ouch...but to be honest, he wasn't the first person to tell me that. That's not exactly what you want to hear when you're in a coaching role, is it? But instead of shutting him down, I listened.

"I mean, I talk to you, and sometimes you don't even respond, or you just brush off what I say."

He had a point. I have a habit of selective listening, zoning out when I'm distracted or when I'm not fully present. It's not ideal, especially for someone who values communication as much as I do. In that moment, I realized I needed to confront my behavior. I had to acknowledge that my lack of presence wasn't just about me—it was affecting the people I cared about. I've since learned that to be a better listener, I either need to give the speaker my full attention, or let them know I'm not fully present at that moment and that I'll circle back to them later. It's about being honest and setting expectations to avoid frustration.

This wasn't the only time I've confronted my blind spots. There was a summer when I was on an unpaid leave of absence while completing my master's degree. I would sit up in the bleachers at the pool with my schoolbag, immersed in my books, barely noticing the world around me. I thought I was disengaging from home life in a productive way. What I didn't realize was the impression I was giving off. One evening, over drinks, Teresa shared, "You know, Tania, when I first met you, I thought you were unapproachable."

I was shocked. Me? Unapproachable? But it made sense. I had been so focused on my work that I hadn't noticed how others might perceive me. I was disconnected, lost in my own world and that caused others to miss the opportunity to connect with me. This was a real eye-opener for me, and another reminder that I had blind spots I needed to address.

These experiences taught me that we *all* have blind spots—areas we don't realize are affecting others or ourselves. The Johari Window, a tool I've used in coaching, suddenly became deeply personal. It is all about finding balance in how much of ourselves we reveal while allowing for the possibility of learning from what others see in us. The more we share about ourselves, the more we allow others to see our true selves. But that is not always easy.

Some things are harder to share—our fears, insecurities, or vulnerabilities… and that's okay. We all choose what to disclose, and it's normal to withhold certain pieces of ourselves. But there is power in being open, in stepping outside our comfort zones, and in trying things we've been scared of. And we'll never know what we're capable of if we don't take that leap.

I think about how often we hold ourselves back from trying something new—afraid we won't be good at it or that we might fail. But I've come to realize that we don't know what we don't know, until we try. Just think about something you've been putting off because it feels too daunting. Now, imagine if you just took that first step. You might surprise yourself with what you learn. And if not, you'll have learned something valuable anyway.

I continue to be surprised all the time by the lesson's life throws my way.

I've stretched myself many times, but there has always been something pulling me to do so—my vision. It is what keeps me moving forward, even when things feel uncertain.

On one of my first vision boards, I placed an image of a woman in a yoga pose. To me, it symbolized peace and tranquility, qualities I deeply desired to invite into my life. A week later, Energie EnCorps fitness studio opened in my neighborhood, offering free yoga sessions for the last weekend in January. My friend Anita called me and asked if I wanted to go.

Who would have thought that at this stage in my life, I'd be stepping into a yoga class? But I went.

I know now why I placed that image on my vision board but I experienced exactly what it evoked in me. The feeling of stillness, of alignment, and peace—it was like stepping into my own vision, the vision I had created but didn't yet fully know how to manifest. And as I write this, I realize how the pandemic has shifted so much of our routines, and it is time for me to return to the studio and reclaim that sense of tranquility.

When I agreed to go to yoga with Anita, I stretched myself in a new direction…physically and metaphorically. I took action on something that had been quietly residing in my vision—and that action brought me the peace I had been yearning for. So, I ask you: What have you been wanting to do but haven't tried yet? Maybe it's time to cross another item off your bucket list or simply stretch yourself from the known.

Speaking of stretching myself, in the fall of 2021, I joined the Emerging Speakers Academy. The academy offers a certification program for speakers, from bronze to platinum levels. I had completed five of the six challenges required for the bronze certification, but there was one that had been holding me back. The challenge was to post a three-minute video on social media, sharing my message in a powerful and authentic way. At first, I couldn't understand why this one was so difficult, after all, I'd created many videos for SweetLegs when I was selling a product. Why was this different?

It turned out the key was getting clear and confident in my message. I had a story, but was I ready to share it in such a public way?

As I pondered this, I realized that the very challenge of creating this video was a reflection of my own growth. In the past, I would have avoided putting myself out there in such an exposed way, but now I saw it as an opportunity to share my journey—how I overcame my fears, doubts, and obstacles to live my truth. I may be doing that a little more each time but rest assured, working through those fears each and every day is a lifelong journey.

Ironically, the message I was struggling to deliver was about overcoming challenges and stepping out of comfort zones. It felt like a full-circle moment. It wasn't just about creating a video; it was about embodying the very lesson I was teaching. Sometimes, the hardest things to do are the ones that will transform us the most.

It was two o'clock in the afternoon and I was so exhausted I just wanted to close my eyes and forget about everything. An hour later, I woke up to the warmth of the sun streaming through my window and I felt a strong pull to step outside. As I inhaled the fresh summer air, I scrolled through my meditation playlist: *A Practice for Focus and Productivity to Manifest a Happier and Healthier Life*. One particular track really caught my attention. Within minutes, I began to bring my attention to a task that had been lingering in the back of my mind for a long time—a task I'd often pushed aside.

Today was going to be different.

I focused all my attention on the task I'd been avoiding. I tuned into how I was feeling—no judgement, only kindness. My mind felt clear, the clutter was gone, and I felt light and free.

As I visualized myself moving forward with the task, I saw it through the lens of compassion. I began to recognize why this goal had been calling me, and with a deep breath, I leaned into it. I thought of the positive benefits I'd experience from completing it—and how it could help others. As I imagined it, I saw it happening before my eyes.

And that is the difference.

When we approach our goals with a fresh perspective, infused with the right energy, we draw closer to making them a reality. Forget about why you haven't done it yet, instead, ask yourself why it is there in the first place. Our dream life and the goals that guide us toward it are one and the same.

So now, bring that goal you've yet to complete into your view, no matter how big or small, no matter how daunting or thrilling. Imagine starting, and say to yourself:

I am proud of me.
I am worthy of all the positive benefits I will receive when I
accomplish this.
I am achieving and living out all of my goals and dreams.

Take a moment to celebrate the sensation of achieving it. Feel the confident vibrations of realizing your goal. And with this new energy and perspective, allow yourself to believe that nothing will hold you back this time.

The final step for me to reach my goal and attain a Bronze Level Certification from the Emerging Speakers Academy was to post an inspirational message on social media. This was it, and it sure felt great: "You just need to see it, believe it, and you will achieve it."

Those words resonated with me back in the summer of 2017 when I was completing my Personal & Professional Coaching Certificate and they still resonate today.

The challenge for that certification was centered around two core competencies in the coaching process…and I wrestled with them.

Take 1:

I had to conduct a coaching session in front of an audience of six people, with two evaluators sitting beside us. Being paired with someone on the spot for evaluation is nerve-wracking, to say the least. I was fortunate to be paired with Brinda, who I had gotten to know and befriend during the program. The session began, and while I didn't cover all six elements of the coaching model perfectly, I thought I did okay.

Did I pass? Not sure. But soon, I'd find out.

When Jim and Madeline began their feedback, I knew the drill – start with the positives. Then came the verdict: "Tania, you did not pass the active listening portion and will need to repeat this part. You have what it takes to be a great coach, you just need to refine this skill."

I felt deflated. I couldn't rely on the same speed I was used to for getting results. I had to stop and reflect: *How could I move forward from here? What lesson was I supposed to learn?*

It was part of my journey. I was venturing into new territory. It would become transformational.

While most of my cohort passed, one or two had also struggled. Brinda couldn't believe it, but deep down, I could.

I knew I needed to practice more and focus more on being with the client where they were at, instead of trying to fix things for them. Coaching is about co-creating with the client. They need to come to their own conclusions, make their own plans, and commit to moving forward. This was so different from teaching or advising. My default approach was always to solve problems—an approach which has no place in life coaching.

When I think back to what Adrian said to me, "Mom, you don't listen very well," I now understand what he meant.

Take 2:

So, I took the summer to practice. But, before doing that, I sent in another coaching session recording that I believed reflected my improvement in active listening. While the attempt was good, I still needed to refine those skills. Coaching doesn't happen overnight.

"Trust the process, Tania, and you'll get there," Jim reassured me over the phone.

I practiced. I was patient. I trusted the process. I did the work.

Determined to succeed, I kept improving with every session. By the end of the summer, I was not only ready, but I felt confident in my coaching abilities.

Take 3:

Yes, I passed! Thank you, Jim. It seems like I needed to fail in order to succeed.

Failure is a natural, unavoidable part of life and yet it is so very hard for us to accept. We don't always want to acknowledge our limitations, or confront the discomfort of not being where we want to be, but if we take the time to process it, to seek the meaning behind it, and see it as an opportunity to grow, we not only learn from it, we also become even more successful because of it. There's something incredibly freeing in accepting the truth of our failures—allowing them to shape us rather than define us.

In life, there are things that happen to us and things we make happen. We need to own the truth behind our failures so that we can create a much more courageous ending. Success is not measured by our talent, but by our determination to put in double the amount of effort until we do succeed. And, most importantly, by learning to accept and believe in ourselves along the way.

Never give up on something you really want, no matter how many takes it takes. Acceptance of where you are in the moment—and of where you've been—makes all the difference in moving forward.

Can you imagine not being able to actively listen in a coaching session? Wow!

Over time, I certainly got better, but I know this is an everyday work in progress because it is something I have always struggled with and probably always will. The thing is, I am aware of my limitations here and know that I can develop and improve this skill the more I practice and stay in tune with my client. The more I work on this, the more I'll become better at listening and engaging—both with others and with myself.

Interestingly, my focused attention tends to more readily come when working with my clients…perhaps because it has to. That means more effort is being made in that situation than when engaging with friends and family. Conscious of this, I know that I still struggle with being fully present with my loved ones. I'm committed to working on this—to staying engaged when my mind strays, and not judging myself for those moments, but accepting that they are part of my ongoing journey.

Me trying to justify the problem: Maybe it's an overload of information? Or just being too repetitive? Irrespective, I know who I am. I forgive myself for the times I fall short and I relish when I excel.

Eight years have passed since I received my Personal & Professional Coaching certification in 2017, and who would have thought I would be recognized by *Influence Digest Media* as one of the top fifteen coaches in Montreal for 2022 and 2023? I guess I must be doing something right. Or maybe, I am finally in the right space!

BREAKING FREE
FROM NORMS

Sometimes letting things go is an act of far greater power
than defending or hanging on.
Eckhart Tolle

Oh, I cannot take it anymore! The endless repetition, the same conversations that lead nowhere, and no real movement—it's exhausting. Doesn't that frustrate you? Whether at work or in your relationships, it's the same story: Ideas are shared, promises are made, and yet, nothing ever changes.

I can be guilty of it too, but here's the thing: I'm a doer. Understanding my personality type has really helped me make sense of this inner drive for change. According to the Myers-Briggs Type Indicator (MBTI®), I'm an ENFP—Extraverted, Intuitive, Feeling, and Prospecting – with a borderline J. That "J," which stands for Judging, isn't about being judgmental; it reflects a preference for structure and decisiveness. It shows up in my need for forward momentum—for goals to be set and actually achieved. I've always found gratitude, no matter the circumstance, and that blend of flexibility with just enough structure explains so much about my path—and why I feel so aligned with the work I do today, in service of others.

What I have realized is that the reason I sometimes feel stuck, unmotivated, or disengaged is because I've been working within a structure that doesn't allow me to fully use my strengths. I want to help create real change, but to do that, I need to be able to exercise my creativity, my skills, and my passion for helping people grow. I thrive when I'm able to work in a way that nurtures the change I want to see in the world—one person at a time.

This is why I'm so passionate about working with individuals to help them discover their own self-awareness. But I also see the bigger picture and the organizations that could truly benefit from this work around awareness. Imagine if workplaces genuinely listened to their employees, not just as workers, but as people with dreams, goals, and values. What if companies didn't just focus on tasks, but took the time to understand what each individual is passionate about and what they aspire to? We'd have a culture of caring, and a community of sharing.

Employees who feel valued, heard, and seen will perform better, and that benefits everyone. So much attention is given to mental health these days, and one of the best ways to support it is by helping people work toward their personal goals. What if we started by seeing employees not as 'resources' but as humans? If we created space for them to share their goals, reflect on their visions, and gain clarity, we'd be fostering a culture of well-being and inspiration.

I've seen the impact of vision board webinars firsthand. Whether in workplaces or community services, these sessions have sparked gratitude, relief, and inspiration. People are empowered when they can create their vision, share it, and take actionable steps toward it. There is something very powerful about helping others connect with their vision, especially in the workplace where it is often overlooked. My heart lies in humanizing the workplace, one person at a time.

Your personal vision shouldn't be a secret. The more you talk about it, the more resources and support you'll gather to bring it to life. As the saying goes, "vision without action is just a dream. Action without vision just passes time. But vision with action, well that's pretty clear, that's how we change the world, at least our world."

Here am I writing this book, but how did I get here?

It started with a five-day 'Write Your Book Outline' challenge in April 2023. A few months later, in July, I found myself at a writing retreat with none other than Rachael Jayne Groover and Datta Groover, who have been instrumental in my spiritual and successful journey. An incredible group of women participated in the retreat where space was created for us to pour our thoughts and words onto paper so they could, eventually, be shared with the rest of the world.

I can still hardly believe it, but this real. My vision is becoming a reality.

And it all began with a Facebook post that seemed tailored just for me, like the Universe knew exactly what I needed to see. It pointed me to Racheal Jayne and Datta Groover, and their approach to trusting the process. Unlike other webinars I've attended, they encouraged me to let my soul guide the journey, before strategy took over. From that moment, I knew I was with the right people. And now, here I am.

LOVE AND RELATIONSHIPS

Let there be spaces in your togetherness,
and let the winds of the heavens dance between you.
Khalil Gibran

People. How do they come into our lives? Do we choose them, or do they choose us? Is it fate? A coincidence? A delicate thread pulling us together for a reason, a season, or a lifetime? I've always believed that everyone enters our life for a reason, but sometimes those reasons don't reveal themselves until years later.

It was December 25, 1980. Christmas Day for most, but not in our house—we celebrated Ukrainian Christmas on January 7. Sure, there might have been a turkey dinner that evening to honor my father's birthday, but the real holiday festivities were still weeks away. For us, that December 25 felt just like an ordinary day.

Which is why I found myself at my best friend Chris' family Christmas celebration. I was sixteen years old, and oblivious to the fact that this ordinary evening would change everything for me.

He was there. Eighteen years old. Her cousin. My future husband.

I wore a simple black dress. I thought was cute but didn't expect anyone else to notice. He noticed. We noticed each other. There was something in the way his eyes lingered a second longer than usual, in the way my heart skipped a beat when he smiled. I was shy—painfully shy—and it showed. But that spark, that moment, stayed with me for years after.

The following spring brought another opportunity. One of my friends was turning sixteen, and we were planning her birthday party. When it came to the guest list, I made sure to add his name. It was intentional. A deliberate nudge to destiny. He had a feeling there was a reason he'd been invited. He was right.

The night of the party, I dressed carefully, choosing a red-and-white sailor dress. I spent what felt like hours curling my long hair, perfecting every strand. I was ready. When the music started playing, he asked me to dance. My heart raced as we swayed to the rhythm, my thoughts swirling with excitement and nerves.

Chris had been nudging me to ask him to my high school graduation, convinced this was the perfect moment. So, in the middle of our dance, I summoned all my courage and asked, "Would you like to take me to my high school graduation?"

No answer.

I froze. Did he not hear me? Did he not want to?

I tried again. "Would you like to take me to my high school graduation?"

Still nothing.

I could feel my cheeks flush as panic set in. Maybe I was being too forward? Or maybe he was playing with me? Determined not to let the moment slip away, I asked one final time, louder this time, "Would you like to take me to my grad?"

He smiled, finally catching my words above the music. "Sure, I'd be happy to take you to your grad."

Relief flooded through me, and I felt the tension melt away. Turns out, he hadn't heard me the first two times—the music had drowned out my soft voice. Sometimes, it really does take a little extra effort to be heard. But I meant it when I told myself I wouldn't ask again. He answered just in time.

On grad night, he was the perfect gentleman. I was smitten. He was charming, handsome, and everything my teenage-self had dreamed of. The night didn't end with the music. My mother hosted everyone for breakfast, and I wished the hours could stretch longer. That magical connection lingered, even as the sun rose the next day.

A week later, he asked me on a date—our first. June 6, 1982. The start of what would become an eight-year courtship.

Fast forward to December 1988. Snowflakes floated gently from the sky as we dined at Casa Napoli, our favorite Italian restaurant. The air felt electric, as if the world itself was holding its breath. All through dinner, I wondered, *Will he ask? Will this be the night?*

The meal ended, the check was paid, and he helped me into my coat. We stepped outside into the crisp winter air, the snow glistening under the streetlights. The city was quiet, peaceful, wrapped in its own magic.

As we passed the large window of the restaurant, he stopped. My breath hitched as he dropped to one knee, right there on the snowy sidewalk.

"Will you marry me?"

It was everything I had ever dreamed of. I barely managed to say, "Yes!" before the entire restaurant erupted into applause. The moment felt like a scene from a movie—the snow, the magic, the joy.

I was going to marry the love of my life.

And on May 26, 1990, I did. It was a beautiful day, filled with the kind of hope and joy that only a wedding can bring.

But life, as it so often does, had other plans. In August 2008, the million-dollar family we had built would once again shatter…one final time.

After the initial shock wore off and he accepted what was happening, it became an amicable divorce—at least as amicable as a divorce can be. Coming to grips with the fact that we were parting ways wasn't easy for either of us. But I wasn't bitter because I knew, deep down, that we were no longer bringing out the best in each other. When that realization hits, you know what you need to do—not just for yourself, but especially for your children.

Walking out of the courtroom on a crisp fall day, the sunlight filtering gently through the trees, the world seemed indifferent to the life-altering chapter that had just closed behind us. As we rode the escalator, he looked at me, his face softened by a rare vulnerability.

"What about Danylo?" he asked quietly. "I want to be buried next to him when I die."

I stopped, mid-step, his words striking a chord so deep that it almost took my breath away. I looked up at him, my voice steady but my heart heavy. "Me too. I guess, in the end, we will be together—with our baby."

For a brief moment, the weight of our grief and love for our precious baby boy transcended everything else. No matter what had happened between us, we would always be Danylo's parents, and together in the end.

After we sold our home in October 2008, I discovered a beautiful, brand-new condominium was being built in a nearby neighbourhood. It felt like the perfect symbol of a fresh start—exactly what my children and I needed. We stayed in our home until June 2009, when it was time to move. Unfortunately, moving into a condo meant that we couldn't bring with us our beloved family dog, Mika. Instead, Mika went to live with my children's father.

Mika had brought so much joy to our lives. In the quiet evenings, she would rest her chin on my ankle, offering comfort and companionship as the children slept. She also got me back into a routine of walking twice a day—something I deeply missed when she was no longer with us. Letting her go was not easy, but I found solace in knowing she was still part of our family. The children could visit her anytime and, in that small way, she remained a connection to the life we were leaving behind.

On June 17, 2009, we became the first family to move into the new condo building on Sources Street in Dollard-des-Ormeaux. It was perfect, not because it was grand, but because it was ours—a space to rebuild, heal, and begin anew.

Once the children and I settled in, I discovered the joy of being my own boss—the sole decision-maker in my life. I cherished the peace and independence that came from having full control, and I knew that reclaiming this space was vital for my healing, and for my children.

Life was good.

Life was really good.

In 2010, I decided to try something new—online dating. Back then, it wasn't as common as it is now, and taking this step felt like embracing my own version of progress. That is how I met Tommy.

At first, our relationship felt like a breath of fresh air. Early in our time together, Tommy lost his job. My friends were surprised that I stood by him, but I did. I saw him through that difficult time, offering support when he needed it most.

One day, during a particularly hard time in our relationship, Tommy called me his 'angel.' It wasn't just a passing comment—it came from a place of deep gratitude. He saw me as someone who lifted him up when he felt most lost, someone who gave without expecting anything in return. At the time, I took it as a heartfelt compliment, but as now I reflect, I realize it may have touched on something deeper—something that feels like it's woven into the very fabric of my being.

But life has a way of revealing what's truly underneath the surface. A few years later, Tommy lost another job. This time, he started considering a career change—he wanted to pursue his passion for music and recording. I encouraged him to follow his dream, though I was surprised when he didn't even try to take a temporary job to ease the financial burden. Over eight months, he meticulously planned a move back to his home country of Panama, where he hoped to start afresh. He asked if I'd eventually join him there but I wasn't entirely sure, even though I had bought a condo there a few years earlier.

That was a space I envisioned as a retreat for us—a place where we might retire, and somewhere my children could visit. I wanted to support his dream, but deep down, I think I was trying to figure out if I could fit his vision into mine. I got in over my head with the purchase, but it felt like the right thing to do at the time.

The months leading up to his departure were revealing. Tommy stayed with me for two months before he left for Panama in August 2015, and while I wished him well, I felt a profound sense of relief the day I drove him to the airport. My body felt lighter, my mind freer, and I realized how much energy he had been taking from me. The sensation was eerily similar to the release I felt after my marriage ended—a clarity that only came when I reclaimed my space.

Three months later, I flew to Panama to visit Tommy. For him, it was a chance to solidify our future together. For me, it was a test—a way to gauge how I truly felt.

The moment that made everything clear happened on a warm December evening by the ocean. It should have been perfect—a romantic proposal under the stars. But when he asked, I felt a heavy wave of unease. I smiled and said "Yes," thinking it was the right thing to do but, deep down, I knew something was off.

The days that followed were filled with doubt and even tears. I finally told him, "I am nowhere near ready to think about an engagement, let alone a wedding. I need to figure things out for myself."

He agreed that I keep the ring as a symbol of commitment, but in my heart, I already knew the relationship was on borrowed time.

Six months later, we broke up. By then, I had already started to disengage and when it ended, I felt an overwhelming sense of relief. My therapist told me, "Tania, you know exactly what you're doing—you just need validation to do it."

She was right. I knew what needed to happen, and by the time I made the decision, I had clarity and peace.

Perhaps that is why freedom resonates so strongly with me. It's not about walking away; it's about understanding when my purpose has been fulfilled. I think of myself as being there to help people rise, to stand on their own, and when my time with them is done, I move on, grateful for the time we shared and the lessons learned. Could this be the work of an Earth angel?

I sometimes wonder if my baby boy, my guardian angel, works through me, guiding me toward a path of giving and letting go. It is a humbling thought, one that reminds me that my love and support come from a place far greater than myself.

My ex-husband often wrestled with this side of me. On one hand, he admired it and would say, "You're so good—I wish I could be as good as you." But on the other hand, perhaps not. He sometimes called me a martyr, as though my willingness to give to others without hesitation was a reflection of something he couldn't quite reconcile within himself.

Looking back, I see now that my role in Tommy's life wasn't to stay forever—it was to guide him through that chapter and encourage him to pursue his dreams. And while our paths diverged, I feel peace knowing I stayed true to my nature. Freedom is my anchor, my guiding star, and perhaps it's part of the gift I carry—a gift that connects me to my ancestors and their legacy of strength, love, and resilience.

Every relationship I've been in has been a lesson, a stepping stone in my journey toward understanding myself and what I value most. Freedom, clarity, and the ability to create a space that feels right for me have always been guiding principles. And while Tommy and I didn't work out, I'll always be grateful for what that chapter of my life taught me.

One thing I've come to understand about myself is that I can love and care deeply, even at a distance. I don't need to be someone's 'everything,' nor do I expect anyone to hold that space for me. That realization has brought me both peace and clarity about the kind of relationships I'm meant to have.

Maybe that's why men in my life have often been quick to want to secure the deal through promises of marriage or visions of a shared future. But for me, with time, that initial excitement often fades. My fairy-tale marriage came once, and while it didn't last forever, it shaped me in ways I'll always cherish. I don't feel the need to recreate it.

It was a hot summer evening in August 2017 when I found myself at an Italian restaurant with a fellow coach. We were both single and navigating the complexities of midlife. Over wine and laughter, we made a bold pact: Why not give online dating another try? After all, what did we have to lose?

The following night, bored and flipping through TV channels, I opened my laptop and decided to create a profile on Match.com. After carefully crafting my bio, I paused. Should I really pay for this? I saved my profile and went to bed.

The next morning, I woke to a flurry of email notifications. My profile had garnered attention even though I wasn't yet subscribed. Intrigued, I caved and signed up.

And there he was—the first match to capture my attention. His warm smile and kind eyes drew me in, and something in his profile resonated deeply. I felt a spark of curiosity, a quiet nudge from the Universe to take a chance.

From the moment Ken and I connected, conversation flowed effortlessly. By midweek, we had planned a coffee date for Friday. But as the day approached, I thought, *why stop at coffee?* Dinner felt more fitting.

We met at Vivaldi's at 7:00 p.m. Ken brought a bottle of wine, and we both brought our best selves. The hum of conversation surrounded us, but we might as well have been the only two people in the room. The aroma of garlic and basil hung in the air, and our laughter flowed as easily as the evening breeze. Before we knew it, the lights flickered—it was closing time.

Neither of us wanted the night to end. Ken walked me to my car, and on a whim, we decided to grab coffee and dessert at Rockaberry Bakery. The hours slipped by as we ate warm apple crumble and ice cream…too soon it was 1:30 a.m.

As he walked me to my car, we shared a brief, sweet kiss. And in that moment, I knew. Fast forward, and we are in our seventh year together.

With Ken, I've started to see that perhaps I can experience both freedom and security, as I once did in my marriage, but this time without the traditional framework of being married. There's a kind of balance that feels possible now—a way to honor my deep value of freedom while embracing the comfort of a steady partnership.

That's not to say it's been an easy journey. Ken has longed for us to unite more fully, while I've held steadfast to maintaining the space I cherish, not just for me, but also for my children. Blending families has never been on the cards for me. At times, this difference has created tension, moments where we've questioned if our paths could continue to align. Yet, despite these challenges, there is a renewed sense of hope as we move forward.

Ken and I have built something unique—a relationship that isn't bound by societal norms but instead is shaped by mutual understanding, respect, and love. In the past, the excitement of commitment often faded for me because it came with expectations that conflicted with my need for space and autonomy. But with Ken, I'm learning that freedom and security aren't opposing forces; they can coexist when two people honor each other's individuality.

Daria, a friend of mine, once said, "Tania, you're still flying like a butterfly, and when you reach my age and retire, you might feel differently about all this."

Her words stayed with me. Perhaps she is right. Maybe, in time, I'll feel differently about merging my life with someone else's, for now though, I am at peace with the way things are.

Each step I've taken—through relationships, challenges, and choices—has been part of my walk to freedom. I started walking daily years ago, seeking clarity and peace. No matter the weather—freezing cold or sweltering hot—I walked. Walking became my ritual, my escape, my way of grounding myself.

And so, I keep walking. And I never feel alone.

ENERGY FOR GROWTH

The people who shape our journey

Some people arrive and make such a beautiful impact on your life,
you can barely remember what life was like without them.
Anna Taylor

No one is meant to walk the hardest paths alone. Just as bridges help us cross what we cannot cross alone, support systems lift us when the weight is too much to carry by ourselves.

Whatever journey we are on in life, one thing I know for certain: we are not meant to travel it alone. Throughout my life, I've been fortunate to build a healthy support network—inspired by David McLean's post where he referred to this as "a *personal board of directors*." Just as organizations rely on a board to navigate challenges, we too need our own circle of trusted individuals. This group includes mentors who offer wisdom, cheerleaders who uplift us, coaches who guide us, and colleagues who walk beside us. It's the group we turn to, no matter what life throws our way.

I am deeply grateful for my personal board, which includes members who have been by my side for over thirty years. These relationships work both ways—we support each other, offering strength, guidance, and honesty when it's needed most. There is real power in being surrounded by those who not only celebrate your victories but also hold space for your struggles.

Life is not meant to be navigated in isolation. We need people who will tell us the truth, even when it's hard to hear, and to offer their hand when we feel like giving up. These loving critics—the ones who nudge us toward growth—are as essential as those who cheer us on. Having a support system is not just a luxury, it's a lifeline. It allows us to stumble, knowing we will be caught, and encourages us to keep moving forward when all we want to do is stop.

In the end, it is not by doing it all on our own that we grow, but through the shared wisdom, love, and guidance of others. A support system isn't a sign of weakness—it's a testament to the strength that comes from choosing to connect, trust, and lean on those who care about us, just as we care for them.

I don't know how anyone could navigate life without a personal board of directors. I am truly grateful to have mine. Nurturing these relationships requires commitment and a belief in the importance of friendships. It is about building solid connections with people and not giving up on them. It says a lot when we can remain in each other's lives in meaningful ways—witnessing one another's struggles and triumphs along the way.

I am deeply honored to have lifelong friends serving as my personal board of directors—cheerleaders who have been with me every step of the way. Their unwavering support and belief in me fuel my growth, both personally and professionally. Each one brings their unique gifts, perspectives, and strength to the table, enriching my journey in ways I could never have anticipated. With incredible individuals like Anna, Luvana, Enza, Terry, and Tina by my side, I have built a solid foundation of trust and encouragement. They challenge me to be better, offer invaluable insights, and, most importantly, remind me that I am never alone in the pursuit of my goals. Their continued support is a constant reminder that growth is never a solo journey—it's a collective effort, driven by the energy, wisdom, and love of those who truly care.

Over time, our boards can evolve, just as we do. We may find ourselves heading in new directions—both personally and professionally—and come across others who align more closely with where we are in life. This is perfectly understandable. However, there comes a time when some people no longer serve us in the way they once did. We need to be mindful of this, because if we stay in the company of those who drain us, it will be difficult to move forward. Their energy will suck the life out of our growth, leaving us stuck. In these moments, we must have the courage to let go and move on. It's not about abandoning people; it's about honoring ourselves and our growth.

Over the years, I have found myself slowly disengaging from friendships. While I was growing and seeking new opportunities, some friends remained stuck in their limiting patterns. I found it difficult to maintain those friendships. And perhaps they found it hard to remain friends with me. That's okay. Some friends are meant to come for a season, a reason, and some, a lifetime. Conversations that were filled with negativity and an unwillingness to change, started to drain me and were difficult to maintain. That's when I realized that I wasn't showing up as my best self in these friendships anymore, and that staying in that energy was holding me back. They weren't easy decisions to make, but I am grateful that those moments happened quite naturally. Slowly, over time, there was less contact and engagement, speaking to the fact that our lives had simply taken different directions. That's okay. I have found new connections that support my growth and challenge me in positive ways, and I feel lighter and more empowered as a result.

Ultimately, we nurture the relationships that are meaningful to us throughout our journeys. Trust me, as long as you have supportive members, ladies and gentlemen, you can get through anything.

Throughout this book, I have shared stories of the incredible individuals who sit on my personal board, and my gratitude for them is immense. These connections have shaped my journey, providing me with strength, guidance, and unwavering support. They serve as a powerful reminder that the people we choose to surround ourselves with can profoundly impact our paths. So, choose wisely.

Take a moment now to consider your directors: who do you have sitting on your board?

PERSONAL BOARD OF DIRECTORS

Everyone needs a team of people, a Personal Board who can provide support throughout your life. The members of your PB don't necessarily know they're on your board and you do not necessarily call all of them every time you need advice. However, having a PB can be critical to your success and your mental well-being.

PEER

Who inspires you with fresh ideas? Who validates your work?

CHEERLEADER

Who encourages you? Who listens while you vent?

CAREER COACH

Who challenges you to become a better you?

YOU

WHO ARE THE PEOPLE THAT HOLD YOU UP?

MENTOR

Who at a senior level supports you? Who is influential?

CONNECTOR

Who can introduce you to others in your profession or industry?

WELLNESS COACH

Who encourages your health & wellbeing?

WHO WILL SIT ON YOUR BOARD?

PEER

CHEERLEADER

CAREER COACH

YOU

MENTOR

CONNECTOR

WELLNESS COACH

Relishing in my mother's ability to choose freedom, I followed her footsteps in belonging to and helping in the community. I wanted to make an even greater impact, so I immersed myself in learning, education, and earning degrees and certifications that not only helped me professionally, but also brought insight into my personal life.

My story is now expanding beyond the basic needs and sense of belonging (Maslow, 1943) to bringing an awareness that we all have the power to make choices and decisions that align with who we are. It is about having hope, as long as we have a tomorrow. And nourishing people's souls by inspiring them to live by what they value (as I have learned to live by mine) while consistently applying my strengths (love of learning, kindness, gratitude, spiritually, and fairness) as much as I can.

Applying our strengths is one thing, deciding on what to do next—what project, goal, or new idea—is another. This is where I can feel stuck, as I believe many others do too. When you have a brain that is in overdrive, how do you decide what to do next, and when?

I had been applying Michael Bungay Stanier's model to determine which goals are truly worth pursuing. The model scores three aspects of a goal on a scale from 1-7: How thrilling is it? How important is it? How daunting is it? According to the model, if your goal scores between 18 or more, that is a goal worth pursuing. (Bungay Stanier, 2016)

You see, goals should ignite excitement and stir a bit of fear, something that counters the feeling of obligation. And, when you think about the impact, the question becomes: Who will this affect, and how?

It's about considering how your pursuit will stretch beyond just you.

I used this model to evaluate my own goal, and here I am, writing a book! It definitely exceeded that 18/21 score. I'm thrilled, excited, and, to be honest, a little scared. Will anyone even want to read it? What will I write next? The uncertainty and nervousness are real, but the weight of it all reminds me: This is a goal worth pursuing.

And here is the best part—I'm not doing this alone. I've shared this goal with my support system, and knowing they're there, cheering me on, makes all the difference. We are never truly alone in life, nor should we be. I rely on my support system—my angels, my family, my friends, and, most of all, my children. Building and nurturing these connections is crucial for our growth and success.

I hope you have your own support system in place, because, trust me, it is the foundation that helps you rise, even when the journey gets tough.

Have you ever heard that we are the average of the five people we spend the most time with? It's an interesting thought. If you reflect on your network, what does that look like for you? For me, I see a beautifully balanced and diverse group of women, each with unique strengths, personalities, and character traits. In many ways, I see reflections of myself in them.

The people we surround ourselves with inevitably shape us. Sometimes, they hold up a mirror to behaviors we'd rather not see in ourselves. When I notice something in someone that I dislike—a behavior I know I'm capable of exhibiting—I take it as an opportunity to pause, reflect, and choose a different course. Instead of falling into that pattern, I remind myself to learn from it and strive to do better.

The people who enter our lives do so for a reason—to teach us lessons, challenge us, and inspire us to grow into better versions of ourselves. It's not about judgment or criticism, it's about awareness and the willingness to evolve.

I once asked someone how their neighbor was doing. Their response was something along the lines of, "Well, she's gained a lot of weight, not many people like her or respect her." I remember thinking, that's not quite the answer I was expecting.

Someone once shared an important lesson with me: When you ask a question, don't have an expectation of the answer. If you know your audience and who you're asking, chances are, you have a good sense of what might come up. So instead of feeling disappointed or frustrated, recognize where the response is coming from and let it go. After all, their answer says more about them than it does about you—and how you choose to respond speaks volumes about your own journey.

I believe living authentically with courage is the ultimate form of individual freedom.

Under my mother's wing, I continue to live with gratitude, carrying the lessons she taught me. One of the most important is that when you give, you receive. The learning I receive is what I want to share, to pass on to others. When you start from a place of abundance, you always have enough. We serve a higher purpose than just ourselves. I learned that bad things happen to good people. Life throws challenges our way—losses, tragic events—but as long as we have life, there is hope for a better tomorrow. It is okay to fail. In fact, failure is essential for growth. Although, I still don't like the word 'failure'—those seven letters, two syllables, carry such a powerful meaning.

My mother was a trooper, raising four children, taking charge of the household, and making ends meet during times when my father struggled with PTSD, all the while coping with the difficulties in her marriage and home life. Despite everything, she remained engaged in our cultural activities and created the community she yearned for. She found creative ways to express herself, build a good life for us, and kept our family together. That was her mission.

History repeats itself, but every time it does, we have the power to change its course and make it better for ourselves and our families.

We need something to guide us along the way.

Hope. And gratitude.

Hope is the function of struggle. We all face struggles. Hope is a way of thinking, and it can be learned. Hope happens when we are able to believe there is more out there, and better things are coming. Hope is what we have in our family, this is what defines us.

The common thread that strings us together is hope and gratitude. Gratitude is not only the greatest of all virtues, it is also the parent of all others. This is what has been rooted in me, and the message I continue to convey and instill in my children, and others, because gratitude transforms our past, our present, and our future.

My evolution into the woman I am today is due to the generations of strong Ukrainian women before me striving for freedom through hope and gratitude. The evolution of freedom in the last three generations has been one of civil liberty, freedom of opportunities, and freedom of choice to pursue ultimate happiness.

My journey is founded beyond my mother and her mother before her. It is about being Ukrainian. We, as a people, remain hopeful and resilient during the most difficult times of upheaval. Even when obstacles seem insurmountable, we never give up on our journey to attain success and happiness for ourselves. This mindset of hope, gratitude, and courage is in our DNA, and it is what keeps us Ukrainians determined to fight for ultimate freedom.

Each generation of my ancestors reached a certain level of self-actualization, working hard and striving to attain a rich and fulfilling life, building on the achievements of those that preceded them.

For my grandmother her priority was to fulfill the basic needs of life: safety, shelter, food, and surviving two wars. Her journey saw her fleeing Ukraine to a freedom-bound country where, through her guiding principles of gratitude, hope, giving back, and sharing whatever she had, she fulfilled those needs… and more. She was a healer in her community, bringing relief to one person at a time…to an entire village.

My mother carried on those principles but took her gratitude even further by delighting in being in a country that offers freedom, opportunity, and community. She was able to be true to herself by making choices her mother never could. She created for herself a sense of belong by immersing herself in the Ukrainian community where she felt appreciated and recognized for all her efforts. This is how she found her true self and purpose, beyond caring for her family.

As for me, I followed my mother's path, working with the community and on my sense of belonging. But I realized I wanted to make a greater impact, so I pursued my helping role professionally and in great depth. My journey, my story, is about how I grew my footprint beyond the basic needs and a sense of belonging, to nourishing people's souls to live freely by their core values, as I have learned to live with mine—freedom, creativity, relationships.

Helping people get past their wounds.

My evolution is to help people experience life's dark moments through light—to recognize that no matter what happens in life, they can overcome challenges and know that there is something greater to accomplish.

I live with gratitude and, under my mother's wing, an acceptance of what is. Life happens—loss, failure, tragic events, but as long as there is life, there is hope for a better tomorrow. I learned that it is okay to fail, to readjust your course in life, even after the most tragic losses of all time…because I had the strength to do so.

My mother demonstrated and showed me that a dissolution of a marriage is not failure, and neither was the loss of my son. It was one of my life's most tragic events but I had a family that needed me, and I them. I had much more to give to the world.

My mother's journey to Canada afforded me opportunities that she never had and that were only possible because I was being raised in a free country. Not only do I live in a free country, I was raised in an environment that allowed me to make choices without judgement or fear, knowing that my parents would be there to support me in any decision I made.

Unbeknownst to me, much of my life replicated my mother's…

My mother nourished her soul by helping the Ukrainian community, providing food, talks, creating masterpiece arrangements, and welcoming parishioners and all kinds of people into the community with love and openness. In essence, being true to herself.

We do not have to be victims of circumstance. Even when all is lost, we can find the silver lining and continue on the road to self-actualization. In fact, in many ways it is transcendence.

Being born to uneducated immigrant parents who fled Ukraine after World War ll, I had to figure my career out on my own: What did I want to pursue? What did I want to do in life? I never really had a direction from my parents, I just knew, from a very young age, that I wanted to be a teacher.

And so, I followed the dream. But not in the traditional way…which speaks to my personality so much. I was always encouraged to learn, and for me to keep going to school was clearly important to my parents, even though they had never had any formal education. They did not have to worry about me, because I embraced learning and education to the fullest, and still do at this age. Learning is ageless, and what better place than immersing myself in higher education?

As an avid lifelong learner, I wrapped myself in education and, after graduating from high school at sixteen, I balanced my studies with work. After all, if I wanted to attend a private secretarial college I had to pay for my own tuition.

Today, I realize how my decisions as a youth—for example, not following the traditional path of entering college full-time after high school—were already very much aligned with my thinking, my entrepreneurial mindset, and my multipotentialite character…a term I have only learned in the last year. As a mutipotentialite I can engage and be interested in more than one thing at a time, and not feel guilty or torn between them, because each one of them brings value to my learning, to my being, and to honoring my true self. In fact, from an early age I have always been able to nurture multiple interests, and even balance them in an effective way. Admittedly, this has not always been easy to do…sometimes it did get the better of me!

In all that I have done, finding ways to earn my own money is something I strove for…even as a little girl. After school, in spring or summer, as soon as the weather would get warm, I would make a delicious jug of cold lemonade and small bags of popcorn, set up a table in front of our garage, and sell my wares to anyone on the street. Does this sound familiar to you? Sometimes I made some money, sometimes barely, but that was okay because I had fun and enjoyed the process of being able to do that on my own.

When my brothers started to deliver newspapers, *La Presse*, *The Montreal Gazette*, *Le Devoir*, or the *Montreal Star*, I couldn't wait to get a route of my own. And as soon as I turned twelve, there I was with my own set of newspapers, strolling around the neighbourhood with my little red wagon ready to earn money while making people happy. I loved being outdoors and taking my time to stroll down the streets, except when it would rain or it got cold…then I wasn't so excited to go out. Sometimes I would take so long—maybe I got distracted by something—that my customers must have really wondered what had happened to their newspaper.

This pattern of earning my own money and having independence, of not relying on my parents, really helped me appreciate everything I had. Never once did I question why I didn't have something. Because, you see, I never felt I was missing anything. And if I wanted something, I knew I could buy it because I would just work and earn it for myself.

Shortly after graduating from high school, I choose to go to the Motherhouse, a well-known private secretarial school run by nuns, located in downtown Montreal. At the time, it was not subsidized by the government and sadly it has since closed its doors.

My parents paid for my first semester at the Motherhouse, but I was responsible for paying the remaining four. That was perfectly fine with me. Unlike most of my friends who graduated from high school, I decided to go to work instead. I got a job as a bank teller at the Ukrainian National Bank and worked there until I began my collegial studies eighteen months later.

Everyone else automatically went to college right after high school, but I chose not to. When I think about it, it didn't even really bother me. I kept up with my close friends and, at that time—almost right after high school—I had started dating the man who would become my husband. I certainly did not feel I was missing anything.

Working full-time and earning money felt great. I continued to work part-time when I started my two-and-a-half-year program at The Motherhouse in 1984. I wanted to find a job, downtown, close to the school, and, lo and behold, I became a part-time salesperson in one of the most prestigious department stores in the heart of downtown Montreal, Simpsons.

Oh, what Simpsons brought to me! It was so much more than just selling and wearing designer clothes — hello, Alfred Sung and Simon Chang — it gave me a lifetime of amazing memories. I was lucky enough to earn an hourly wage plus commission. OMG! How great was that? If only I could have held on to it longer than it took to deposit, or kept it in my bank account long enough to earn interest.

I loved making money, but I *loved* spending it even more. I mean, really, how could you not? I was working in a seven-floor department store with so many things to buy. And not just for me…it was nice to get the discounted rate for my family and friends.

One amazing purchase was a beautiful twelve-piece bone China set of dishes that our family bought for our mother. I personally played more of a role in that purchase than just providing the discount…because I knew that, one day, it would be mine. My sister Lida already had picked her set but I never really considered owning one, despite being on the same path to the altar as my sister.

It really was the first China set my mother ever owned. She was so proud. In her day, my mother was a great cook, but when the holidays came everything tasted so much better. You know why? Because it was being served on those gorgeous China dishes.

My brother Walter loved helping our mother set the table when our family would gather for the holidays. The holidays are just not the same anymore. Our family may have grown in number—my two surviving siblings, Lida and Zenon, each have two children, and my deceased brother, Walter, a son— but it seems like, one by one, we have lost members of our family to serve a higher purpose, and Zenny and Lida now live far from our hometown of Montreal. But one thing that I can hold on to, and always have—besides the dishes that appear in my home twice a year at Thanksgiving and Christmas— is the memories and the new tradition of my son Adrian graciously setting the table with those exact same dishes. You see, he is still the one living at home with me.

Simpsons brought me much more than just wonderful purchases and fun experiences, it created a space for me to meet new friends and, believe it or not, many of them still remain in my life almost forty years later. Wow! And, when I think about it, it is quite remarkable how the Universe managed to bring some of these phenomenal ladies (Daria and Marguerite) back into my life after all these years, while others never ever left my corner. I think back to all our suppers and twenty-minute breaks congregating on the fourth floor, savoring our deep conversations while feasting on the best burgers and French fries. Oh, is it time already? Do we have to leave? Let's stay a little longer. Thank goodness we didn't always work in the same department. Sometimes we were in different departments, but when we happened to be grouped close to each other, oh boy, did we have fun. We didn't need to wait for a break to share a story or two, we found those moments in the back room, in the dressing room, or right there on the floor by the cash register.

What a job! What an experience! What a great life!

If only it could always be that way, but all good things come to an end. Simpsons closed their doors in 1989. Converting most of their stores to Simons and others, they vanished from the Greater Montreal directory. Today, thirty-four years later, as I walk through the floors of Simons, I reflect on the good times, the memories, and all the people that I met, including those who continue to be in my life. It is a happy space for me, one that instantly fills my heart with joy and gratitude for having experienced those moments right there in that building. They are moments that will live on and cannot be taken away from me. No matter what they call it now, or who owns it, it will always be Simpsons to me.

I embraced all I learned through my work experiences and found joy the opportunities I was given. When I was no longer having fun or enjoying my work or the environment, I knew it was time to move on. And I had no issue with that—it fed my personality and drive to learn more, do more.

After graduating from the Motherhouse, I worked in the private sector for three years at two law firms and an accounting firm. While working, I was attending night classes on a part-time basis, pursuing my Bachelor of Education, Continuing Education.

I was about two years into the program in January 1990 when I met Luvana in my Business Law 1 class. We instantly connected and quickly became friends. Not only did Luvana become one of my closest lifelong friends, she also encouraged me to apply for a position at the university where she worked.

At the time, I was employed at Thorne, Ernst & Young, an accounting firm, and preparing for my wedding in May. Luvana and my bond grew so strong that I invited her to my wedding and, from then on, we spent more and more time together.

The following winter, in February 1991, an administrative position opened in the Faculty of Law at McGill University. I applied and got the job. Leaving the private sector, where I never truly felt I belonged, marked the beginning of an incredible thirty-year journey filled with both career growth and personal fulfillment.

Why not combine studying and working within the same institution, under one umbrella, in an environment that fostered my growth as a lifelong learner? It was the perfect scenario. And I absorbed every lesson taught, and embraced every opportunity offered, as a earned my two degrees and built my twenty-five-year career at McGill.

Timing is everything, isn't it? Who would have thought that after all these years, I would still be connected to McGill University, and have Luvana as a permanent member of my personal board of directors? We have shared thirty-five years of friendship, a bond that is priceless. More than just friends, we are like soul sisters, connected by an unexplainable force, strengthened by all we have lived through together.

Throughout my time at McGill, I remained curious, interested, and disciplined so I was able to simultaneously pursue both my academic pursuits and my career goals. Going to school at night, I dove into the learning, applying that knowledge to my work and personal life as much as I could. It is not in the theory where we learn the most, it is in the application of the theory in real life. Doing assignments and projects, working in teams, conducting research, all gave me insights I could never have imagined. And it continuously nourished and fed my soul like nothing else did.

I learned how to operate within a large institution, how to harness my strengths, and I constantly found opportunities to leverage my learnings and skills while helping others navigate theirs. Wearing multiple hats was enriching for me. Whether I worked in the personnel office, taught English to technicians at Bell during my lunch hour, or sold products, I exercised all my strengths and all parts of my brain.

I had multiple interests and pursuits throughout my career, but it was only after I stepped off the professional ladder that I realized I had never really embraced a traditional career path. And that is okay. Who says you have to?

Reaching higher level positions was great in one way, but did it really satisfy me? During our thirties and forties, we strive to move up, and sometimes we do so for the wrong reasons: for a title, the prestige, and, of course, the salary. When I held higher positions in the university, I realized they did not actually make me happy. Additional responsibilities that did not align with my interests or strengths ended up making me less motivated, and hence I was not as productive nor as passionate as I might have otherwise been.

The higher you rise in an organization, the less flexibility you have in your own work. Managers and directors need to meet certain objectives while managing teams of employees. Where is the fun in that?

And let's face it, organizations have agendas and missions that need to be respected and followed. Creativity, which may seem attractive in your profile, often does not fare well nor have a place at the higher levels of an organization.

At that point, when you finally reach that higher position that you have been striving for, then you have stop and ask yourself: Does this role bring me satisfaction in my work? Are my strengths and skills being valued and exercised in such a way that bring some joy?

The answer lies within you. Throughout my life, I have accepted what is... not that I didn't try to make changes here and there, when I had the power to do so. But ultimately, I felt powerless in such a large institution to make the meaningful changes I wanted to make, because I always cared more about the people rather than the process.

So, when I chose to step off the corporate ladder, I knew I would never get back on. I want to excel at my 'out of the box', non-traditional calling where I can thrive by doing work that offers me freedom and flexibility—work that I feel driven to do—rather than stay confined in a box.

I am making work—work for me.

In March 2022, while vacationing with Ken, I received a message on LinkedIn from my former boss, Johanne, asking if I was interested in returning to the university—after ten years—to work on a specific project: implementing a post-pandemic interim flexible work arrangement program. After several conversations, I agreed to provide consulting work on a part-time basis, advising three days a week. It was supposed to be a six-month commitment, which was extended twice.

This experience gradually morphed into something more meaningful for me—aligning with what I truly want to be doing: sharing my knowledge through facilitating visioning workshops and guiding people on journeys of self-discovery to help them uncover the work that makes them come alive.

As I continued to write this book, I made the conscious decision in the fall of 2023 not to renew my contract after the Christmas holidays. It was a huge risk—not having the stable income I was accustomed to for my entire career—but it felt right. And that feeling alone was enough to reassure me I had made the right choice. I was finally aligned with who I am and what I want to be doing—freely—creating space for more collaborations while still keeping McGill close to my heart, but at a distance.

And then, my relationship with the university came full circle in an even more meaningful way. I now teach career planning on a contractual basis, bringing a holistic approach to career development that speaks to my whole being. This new chapter allows me to merge my background in teaching with my lived experiences at an institution where I both earned my degrees and built my career. Best of all, I am able to teach in a way that feels true to me, shaping a learning environment that aligns with my values and what I believe in.

THE POWER OF CHOICE

We are our choices.
Jean-Paul Sartre

In life, we tend to return to our knowns—our default takes us there. We are familiar with those surroundings and, at a certain age, we like familiarity. However, when you return with a different perspective—looking from the outside in—you are better equipped to know and decide if you are meant to be there and when you should leave.

In reality, I feel I have always been able to do that, to know when it is time to change. I may have moved between departments and changed roles and positions, but I remained in an institution that aligned with my values, with what was important to me in achieving my goals, in an environment that facilitated my achievements. That is how I succeeded—by leveraging all the skills and resources available to me to excel while demonstrating my loyalty and commitment to the mission, to McGill, to the institution of learning.

But, as with any successes, there were many failures along the way. I may have always steered my career, navigating my ship by making choices that worked for me, but there were times when that ship lost its drive—it didn't move, it stayed still.

I got blindsided.

In 2009, I accepted a position based on ego—the title, the salary, the prestige. My decision to trek up the hill to the Faculty of Medicine, proved to be more than I could handle. That decision would eventually not only see me go back down the hill, but to cross St. Catherine Street to a sister institution.

How could I step into the role of Manager, Academic Affairs so soon after returning from leave, especially while transitioning into a brand-new position in Human Resources as an Organizational Development Advisor? Yet, I did.

What was I thinking? In terms of work process and climate, I entered a completely new landscape. The faculty is somewhat of a unique entity embedded in the university, and it has its own set of standards and rules. After all, it is Medicine.

The learning curve was huge, and one that I began to realize in no way interested nor excited me. I loved the people, but that is not enough when you take on such a role. The responsibility was huge. I was so removed from doing what I enjoy most, and having to resolve problems every day, following processes that seemed so archaic to me, began to reflect in my demeanour and ability to carry on. It was like I was there physically but not emotionally. It is no wonder that in 2012 I made the very bold move to leave the university altogether and pursue a new role in organizational development at Concordia University.

What I have realized most in my career journey is how great a part our work environment plays in our productivity and overall career success. Being in an environment that is conducive to good performance is key...but not always easy to find. It is not just about location, furniture, and space; it is about the leadership, the people you will work with and support, and, most importantly, it's about the work you are actually doing.

There is no perfect place to have all of that, but it does come down to what environment will allow you to show up, to be you, to do the work you love to do, and be supported along the way. That is where you want to be.

It is all about the choices and decisions we make.

But how do you make a decision? What is it based on? How many of us make decisions that we don't really want to make, or don't make the ones we really want to? Have you ever had a great idea for a project you want to start, or something that has been nagging at you for a while, but you just haven't had the chance to focus on it?

I was thinking the other day, naturally during one of my walks, how we make the choice to prioritize certain things in our lives. Hmm, should I add this to my life? God knows I keep adding and adding. Instead of actually saying yes and pursuing it right off the bat, how about a casual "give it a go, give it a try, Tania" to lessen the anxiety around choosing?

It is a lot easier to pursue something when we view it as exploration, like an experimentation rather than a binding contract.

Most of our choices are not permanent, and choosing one thing does not necessarily preclude you from choosing other things. Once you start and dive in, you might love it for years to come…or not at all. You might completely lose interest in it and, guess what? It might even lead you somewhere entirely new. You can never know in advance, so give it a go.

When I connected with Joze on LinkedIn, I never imagined it would lead me to the Grand Slam—the finals of Speaker Slam…but it did. Joining Speaker Slam in November 2021 led me to write this book. It started with just one speech, one story—and lots of encouragement, plenty of support, nights of practice and writing, collaborations with my coach and mentor, and lots of love from my family, friends and the Speaker Slam community. And I not only wrote a speech, but it came in the top ten, and then was awarded third place by the judges.

While realizing my projects and goals can impact many around me—from my family and friends to anyone out there who needs to hear my message and learn from my sharing—I know that they are also part of my personal life journey. I also know that in every journey there are our supports, and I feel fully supported. I always have.

Even when I was a child, I had my siblings with me, and even though I was the youngest, and probably did not get that much attention, I did manage to get what I needed from them to make me happy. I knew from a young age that my happiness came from within. I do not need anyone else, or look for anyone, to fulfill that for me. Maybe that is why I remain happy today, despite everything that happened in my life. I know what it feels like to be happy, to be content. I know what does and does not fill my cup.

Is that a gift I was bestowed with from an early age? Where did this inner contentment come from? Was it deliberate? How did I know to be happy? I am not sure if I will ever really be able to explain it. In fact, sometimes I feel that people don't always appreciate my positive outlook and energy, but increasingly I realize that that is about them and not me.

It's okay for me to be the way I am, seeing the glass half-full and never straying too deep into the negative ruminations that can take one down a rabbit hole. Just the other day when I was working with my coach on the design of my program, she said to me, "Tania, you always go into solution mode even when I try to stay in the negative. It's like you just naturally flow there."

That truly is a gift. But can this be a curse as well? Going into solution mode doesn't always work, and it is not always appreciated…depending on who you are with and what the desired outcomes are.

I learned that the hard way when I was working toward my coaching certification. I realized that my approach would fail in a line of work where I am not to be offering solutions, rather listening to understand while providing space for clients to come up with their own solutions. That was indeed hard for me. I realized I really was not an active listener who stayed attentive to a client, and that was really hard for me, not only to accept, but also to overcome.

Just as learning to truly listen was a challenging but vital step in my personal growth, I have come to deeply appreciate the irreplaceable support and presence of my family throughout my journey.

My siblings, especially my sister, have all played active roles throughout my life—right from my pretend teaching days to my personal and professional achievements and, of course, in my tragic losses and failures. Even when we no longer lived in the same city, they were there to uplift me and make me smile. Technology is great, but nothing can replace the hugs or sharing of laughter and good times that happen when we are together in person. I sure wish it would happen more often. Family lunches and holiday celebrations in a home full of laughter and joy no longer occur. All we have left are the memories, which I will forever cherish.

I sure do miss the vibe I felt with my siblings, simply joking and laughing at the dinner table, or performing—dancing and singing on stage—as we traveled across North America. We even performed at the World International Dance Festival. How many people get to perform with their siblings?

I loved being with them and sharing our heritage with the world. Those were the days I cherished most in my youth, the sense of belonging in my family and community at large. This was the work of my mother, mostly. To instill the love of our culture in every possible way. And we, wholeheartedly, not only embraced it, but were also quite good at it.

Growing up, my older sister Lida and I shared a room and I have to admit we got along really well. In fact, we never really fought. I witnessed and heard many horror stories of sibling rivalries. Our friends across the street, would pull each other's hair or scratch one another with their nails, while Lida and I tried to hold them apart. We never fought like that.

The extent of us being angry with each other—or, more accurately, me being angry with her—was nothing worse than using a skipping rope to divide the room into two with the command, "Now you stay on your side and I will stay on mine." Well, that worked for a while, until I had to leave the room…the door was on her side!

But honestly, our relationship was good, and it worked—it always did and still does. Now, living miles apart, when it feels like the right thing to do, it is easy to disengage by ending our phone call. And then, when we are ready, we simply re-engage.

I sure do miss those days, and I am super grateful for them. Even though we are only a phone call away, and I am surrounded by friends and family, I do feel the distance. Lately, my mother has been saying how lonely she feels these days. And in some ways, I do too. We are the only two left here in Montreal.

Perhaps that's why, when opportunities arose to connect and contribute, I felt called to say yes—even when my first instinct was to say no.

In the Spring of 2022, I was invited by the West Island Women's

Community to deliver a six-week course for women on personal/career development. Initially I was going to say no, wondering how I could deliver such a course. Deep down I knew I had plenty of material: strategies and tools from experts in the field; knowledge I gained throughout my own career; personal experiences I lived through; and insights I gained from my own self-awareness journey and career transformation.

In the end, I decided to say yes. I committed to it. I titled it 'Embark on a Self-Awareness Journey: Discover your unique imprint that fuels your passion for work!'

Even though I had always found ways to share my knowledge—be it through one-on-one coaching or by facilitating workshops—I had never quite put a course together like this one. So, I dug deep into all my content, books of notes, articles, et cetera, and I designed a six-week course. Each week, for one-and-a-half hours, participants would be taken on a self-awareness journey to discover a unique imprint for work that made them come alive. The workshop was designed for women who felt stuck, disengaged, or unsure as to what direction they wanted to take in their personal/professional life. It was to be a place where they could gain clarity and unveil what truly fuelled their passion for work, transforming them from not just 'doing' to 'living an intentional life' with purpose and happiness.

To bring their best selves forward, I really wanted—needed—them to explore the pillars of self-awareness and learn how to better align their values and strengths with insights gained from their 'a-ha' or 'oh no' moments. Because this is what I had experienced as I transformed into the woman I am today, always striving to align whatever I do with my core values and strengths.

Of course, to create the course which, frankly, flowed naturally and beautifully, I had to share what had worked for me in my journey, bringing in some fabulous tools and resources, including 'Insight into Self-Awareness,' The VIA Institute's 'Character Strengths,' and Sparketype testing. I was surprised by how well it went, probably because these ladies really needed both the content *and* the space to share with one another their learnings, challenges, unhappiness in work and life, their sense of loss, et cetera.

In fact, when the six weeks were over, they wanted more, so I thought: *Why not deliver a visioning workshop? They can use their creativity and come full circle by designing their personal vision of what they want to achieve and how they want to be in their lives.*

Unfortunately, we had to wait until after summer for that one, but it did make me realize how many people are struggling. Women, in particular, are struggling to find themselves and reacquaint themselves with the child within who they lost as they became conditioned to believe who they should be and how they should act—inherited cultural beliefs and expectations around their roles as they progressed through lives as daughters, wives, mothers, employees, caregivers, and even widows, just to name a few.

These are real challenges that women face, and while there is no quick fix or one-size-fits-all solution, the one thing we can control and gain insight into is ourselves. Understanding who we are, what we value, who we want to become, and how we want to show up in the world, not only benefits our own well-being, but also influences others, as they too are impacted by our actions and decisions.

Coming to work happy is important to me, always. Of course, I'm not so naïve as to think that happiness is guaranteed every day, but can it be? Stay tuned for more on that later. Doesn't everyone want to feel happy at work? After all, we spend so much of our lives there. If work isn't a place where we feel content, engaged, valued, or safe, then it's not the right place for you or me...or anyone, for that matter.

In my twenties, as a newlywed I landed a great job in the corporate sector at a prominent financial institution. French was important in the role, and although it was my third language, I felt comfortable enough to give it a try. I figured the risk would be worth it. My motto has always been: There is always room for improvement, and every opportunity is a chance to learn.

I began work and everything seemed to be going pretty well. It was a relatively new office—a beautiful space with lovely furniture—and the slow pace of work was not what I was used to, but I was learning and I was curious. Since there was mostly only two of us in the office at any time, I found it quite lonely, but the ambience was very professional, albeit somewhat cold. I loved wearing suits and dressing up for work. I took pride in how I showed up for work every single day, not so much for others, but mostly for myself. And it was noticed. Little did I know how much…

As we gathered around the people who came to celebrate the opening of the new division, I was wearing a beautiful red two-piece skirt suit. Everyone was happy and in a good mood, sharing laughter and holiday cheer. At one point I found myself the only woman in a group of men, when I overheard one guest say to the vice president of the company, "What a lovely assistant you have. Has your wife met her yet?" Everyone in the group smiled and laughed as we carried on with the celebrations.

Well, yes, I *had* already met his wife, but in my naivety, I didn't quite understand the insinuation of that comment at the time…but I would.

One morning shortly thereafter, I was in the kitchen pouring coffee for both the vice president and myself, when he walked in. As he lifted the cup to his lips, he noticed a faint mark of lipstick on it. Pushing it away, he said, "I think this is your cup, Tania. I wouldn't want to taste your lipstick—not off a cup, anyway."

I froze for a moment…perhaps longer…who knows? My heart started pounding and I felt tension and heat all over my body. I forced myself to smile and chuckle a little. I have wondered if he really noticed my reaction because I am known to be an open book—honestly, you can read me so easily. I am not good at hiding my emotions.

I returned to my desk and I knew, right then and there, that this was not the place for me. I could no longer work there. I needed to leave. I never approached Human Resources, or anyone else at head office, for that matter, but that night I wrote up my resignation letter, and the following day I gave my two weeks' notice.

The day I handed the letter to the vice president, he read it with disappointment and said, "You know, Tania, your French was not really on par for our needs, so it makes sense for you to move on and find something that you are more suited for and happy with."

I'll say!

And in my mind, I said, "Oh yes, and as far away from you as possible, that's for sure!"

That was the most short-lived work experience of my career, save for my summer jobs. I lost three months which I would never get back, but as soon as I left other doors opened—widely and welcomingly—leading me to a rich and fulfilling thirty-year career at McGill University.

I listened to my body. I acted on it. I did not feel shame nor guilt. Something was not right, it did not feel right, but I made it right for myself. Could I have done something else about it? Perhaps, but at that time, I just wanted to get out and to move on.

I *was* young and inexperienced, but age had no bearing on my decision. I listened to my intuition and did the right thing for me.

You see, your intuition never lies — but your mind often does. In that moment, choosing to trust my gut served me well, and that was the most important thing at the time. This is exactly what I share with the women in my workshops: listen to your body, trust your gut, because your mind will often try to trick you into believing something else. How many of us truly act on our intuition or trust it fully? That is part of taking ownership of your life — and of yourself.

Sadly, so many women feel they can't take ownership of their lives. They are always putting themselves last, because "I have to do this, I need to do that." We are all guilty of that, but there needs to be a time where you stop and ask yourself: What do I need? What do I need to let go of? How can I nourish myself so that I can continue from a cup that is not empty all the time?

One of the first things the flight attendant says as we wait for our flights to take off is: "Kindly place the oxygen mask over your face before assisting others."

Simple, logical…so then why do we not do this in real everyday life?

Short answer: Because we are often conditioned to put ourselves last.

But what happens when we do this continuously?

We become resentful, overwhelmed, and lose sight of who we truly are. We end up living on autopilot, without purpose.

How long can we sustain that?

Long-term sustainability—that is the issue I want to clarify for women! I want to show them that, while it's important to care for others and fulfill their responsibilities, they must prioritize the nurturing of their inner being before they focus on the doing and going.

Being aligned with what truly matters to you is key to nourishing your soul. And when your body, mind, and soul are properly nourished, look out world…a new you will emerge. The YOU that deserves to be seen, felt, and experienced by the world.

I say it takes steps…baby steps, even. But every step is a step. Imagine a step in the right direction every single day: that's 365 steps every year. That's considerable progress!

Knowledge (learning) and tools are only as good as the way you apply them. I learned that a long time ago. Book-based knowledge can get you so far, but it is in the practice, the experience of it, where we learn and grow the most.

Upon reflection, developing and delivering that course for the first time was not only a fabulous experience for the participants, it was also of great value for me. Week after week, never missing a class, those women trusted me as we journeyed together and created a community of sharing. And I discovered so much about myself in the process. When you commit and put your mind to doing something, something that is meaningful to you and that has a greater impact on others, that is something worth pursuing. I stretched myself beyond my comfort zone, putting hours of work into course design and then spending even more hours with those women, for what might be considered a very minimal financial return. But the real return on this investment would segue into something even greater than I could ever have imagined: Validation that I am doing exactly what I am meant to be doing and enjoying every moment of it. And that is the icing on the cake.

WHO AM I?

To know thyself is the beginning of all wisdom.
Socrates

The journey to get here wasn't always as smooth as I would have hoped. It may not have been quite the same journey of survival as it was for my parents, or my grandparents before them, but it was not a journey without its own challenges—challenges that I had to navigate to experience the freedom I enjoy today.

It took me quite some time to narrow down my core values. I remember when I found myself embarking on my coaching and consulting practice back in January 2021, I worked with Lisa who made me go through a values exercise. I found having so many choices and words to pick from was overwhelming. So many of the values listed resonated with me. *How can you choose only four or five? Really?*

Narrowing them down to 'super values'—four or five main values— seemed easy but really wasn't. Using my creativity, I found a way to cluster several of them into four quadrants. Those that spoke to me were Happiness, Success, Love, and Strength. Within each of those quadrants I listed three or four values that spoke to them. For instance, Happiness for me encompassed gratitude, honesty, purpose, meaning, kindness, and independence. Those are the things that represented happiness for me. You see what I mean…not easy.

This would not be the last of my values exercises. Fast forward to September 2023—by then I had honed in on my values and was able to identify the three overarching super values that I live by: Freedom, creativity, and relationships.

You see, our values can change over time, depending on where we are in our lives—what act, what phase we are living. But even though that may be true, what I also discovered is that if you reflect on your childhood and your life, you can identify moments when you felt really good and really confident in the choices you made. That is when you were living your values and being true to yourself.

When the things that you do and the way you behave match your values, life is pretty good, and it sure leaves you with feelings of satisfaction and contentment. Reflection on the times you were happiest should come from both your career and personal life to ensure some form of balance. My revelation of the importance of freedom in my choices came to me as early as six years old, from a story my mother recently shared that brought it full circle for me.

Growing up in a Ukrainian household and community, Saturdays were very important to our family...particularly for my mother. For my sister and I, Friday nights would be sitting on the living room floor getting our hair curled up so that we would look really pretty for school the next day. Yes, school—not our Monday to Friday English school, but Ukrainian School. Saturdays for me meant Ukrainian School for three to four hours, followed by a Plast (Ukrainian Youth Organization), and then Ukrainian Dancing with the Marunczak Dance Ensemble to end the day.

Unlike most of my friends, who got to sleep in and enjoy Looney Tunes, I was lucky if I caught a glimpse of a cartoon early in the morning, and then only if I finished my breakfast on time.

That was often a struggle. It was tough enough having to stay quiet and listen to teachers for five weekdays, but then there was another half-day of more classwork. Yet, despite all that, I didn't mind going. I enjoyed being with my friends and it was a tight-knit community with whom I always managed to find ways to have fun—whether it was passing notes, tickling each other's arms during history class, or daydreaming. Scouts were fun, too—interactive and full of activities like singing, crafts, and learning Plast values and traditions in preparation for summer camps. After Plast, we headed back to the auditorium for Ukrainian dancing.

Our mothers would gather together in the school auditorium, doing what mothers do best—catching up, talking, organizing and planning events, while their children moved from one activity to another. When the school bell rang, the doors would fly open. Yes! An hour to be free to run around, play, have our snacks. Always wanting to play school, you would find me in the washroom doing just that. It was a big washroom, with plenty of room to play. And if not playing school, hide-and-seek was be just fine.

All the kids knew when it was time to form a circle and start our first movement dance—kind of like a warm-up dance with steps to get the juices flowing, eventually leading into quicker dance movements. I was already in flow, playing, and completely oblivious of the time, when suddenly I heard the first melody of the record playing on the turntable. Then, out of nowhere, I would appear, the studio doors would fly open, and I would run to my spot in the circle. Feet in ballet position, arms wide open, head held up high, I was ready to dance. Almost late, but in fact, just on time.

Wow, that explains so much about me and who I am! Create the space, let me come in, and I will be there. Especially if it is something that I love and is meaningful to me. But try to confine me in a corner, in a box, and I will eventually break free. Not because I don't like being in a box, or the structure, but because it just doesn't speak to who I am. I need to be free to make a choice.

Over the years, I have learned how to live by this value in both my life and career. While there have been times that I needed to be in the box, I always managed to make it work by bending the sides a little to make room to breathe…until I couldn't. And that was okay because usually by then I was ready to come out of it.

When I think of this story, I can't help but feel there are similarities to my mother's sense of freedom. Despite not having much growing up, being in the third youngest of seven, she found joy in the simple things in her life and always managed to do what she wanted to do, and creatively, I may add.

From an early age, she demonstrated her creativity in what she was able to make, and how made people feel through her words—be it performing in plays on stage or giving speeches at the church hall. That talent and strong sense of self permeates through the generations of women in my family, so it is little wonder that my second super value is creativity.

It is that sense of imagination that enables us to create something out of nothing, or bring into existence something new, or express ourselves and our ideas in new ways. In fact, creativity is going beyond the usual, stepping outside of the box...there we are with the box again. Finding new ways to explore ideas or solve issues is just how we experience life. And I have come to learn that creativity is also being open to reinventing yourself, over and over again—to allow yourself to immerse into a new passion and give it your all.

My mother, and her mother before her, may not have had any schooling, but they didn't need schooling use that side of their brain that they were blessed with. It is almost as if, through their creativity and freedom, they experienced happiness and joy. It doesn't matter that happiness and joy for them was so different to what it is for my daughter and me today.

For my mother and grandmother, it was never about pleasing just themselves, it was also always about how they could make a difference in the lives of others. Giving was a word that was etched in their blood, and being grateful for all that they had was key. Because they never really needed to want for more. It just came to them. Recognition, accolades, kind gestures, and proclamations from the community became a common thing for my mother, motivating her even more to continue to share her gifts with the world.

Which makes me wonder: What truly drives people like us? Why are we driven to extend ourselves beyond our families, to help anyone that needs us? Because, yes, we do have lots to offer but, even if that is who we are, the continual giving and sharing can become challenging at times. When does it become about you? When does it become about family? When does it become about others?

Can this need to share, to help, to give, to bring joy to others, ever really be contained in one silo?

There is something to be said about masking—not talking about issues or challenges that are not positive or happy experiences. I would simply compartmentalize them, put them in a box, or avoid them altogether. This seems to have been my way of dealing with the uncomfortable. It is like my mind refused to stay in the sadness, unsure how to talk about it. It just seemed easier not to. And, despite being such a happy person, I did experience great moments of sadness. I would simply avoid bringing up those times and not talk about them…until I did. And it was such a relief when I did.

One September, my friends and I decided to rent an Airbnb for a girls' weekend. Our first night was a lovely evening, the beautiful fall colours surrounded us as we sat by a fire Tina made, enjoying our marshmallow sticks dipped in Baileys…oh, that was yummy. One of the girls suggested we play Truth or Dare, and so we did. A few stories were shared, we laughed, and then it was my turn.

I spoke of a truth. My father was not at my wedding, and it was not because he was ill. The truth of the matter was that he was patiently waiting in his apartment for our neighbour, Mr. Sidaway, to bring him his suit. You see, by this time my parents were separated in their own unconventional way, but why he was not at the house getting dressed like he did nine months earlier when my sister got married, I will never really know. I was too busy getting myself ready and, with the commotion in the house, I didn't realize how time was passing. Mr. Sidaway, unbeknownst to him, went to the wrong apartment building. He went door to door, but he couldn't find my father who was in the building next door…just waiting. Meanwhile, I was being driven to the church in a limousine thinking my father would be giving me away…instead I was escorted by my eldest brother.

Tears rolled down my cheeks as I opened up to the girls about how painful that was for me. After the fact, I realized I didn't do enough to make sure that he was there. I blamed myself. And when I sat with my father to show him my wedding album, I could see the tears rolling down his face, and mine too! There was not one picture of him, of us. How could he not have been at my wedding?

We never really spoke much about it after, because, you know, we don't really talk about our feelings. But we both knew and felt the tremendous void. And as I write this story thirty-three years later, tears are rolling down my face. I know I am forgiven, but what should have mattered the most that day somehow got lost with all the hoopla of the celebration. The notion of out of sight, out of mind certainly held true that day. If I could only turn back time! But I can't, no one can. I know nothing can bring that moment back, and so I let it go. Not having a picture of Daddy with his little girl on her wedding day crushed me. But what I have instead is his unconditional love and all the memories we created together—me growing up and then watching him light up with joy at the sight of his grandchildren—his first granddaughter, Larissa—just as he had when I was born.

That's what I have. The connection, the love, and the beautiful memories.

Another memory that recently came flooding back is a story my mother shared during one of my visits. She recalled how Tato would take my sister Lida and me to the park. You'd think we'd be dressed in play clothes, ready to get messy in the sand. But no, Tato had us dolled up in our pretty dresses and shoes. I was in the stroller and Lida walked beside me, all dressed up like we were going to a party rather than the playground.

When we got to the park, Tato would sit us both in the swings and push us, over and over, until we asked him to stop. Knowing him, that probably took longer than we wanted! But he did it with such quiet dedication. Then, when it was time to leave, back in the stroller we went…back home again.

Pretty in the Park, that's what I call it.

It speaks volumes, doesn't it? About his love, his care, and maybe even his pride. Perhaps, without ever saying a word, he was teaching us how deeply we mattered—to him and to the world. Maybe that's why, to this day, how we present ourselves still matters to us. It was never about vanity; it was about honoring those moments, the effort, the love.

And in that swing, in those little shoes, in the way he showed up, *I was loved*. We both were.

NEVER FORGOTTEN

A Lifelong Connection

Guardian Angel

An angel formed of purest love
Is sent to you from God above.
Ever watchful and always true,
An angel meant for only you.

ROOTS OF RESILIENCE

Like branches on a tree, we all grow in different directions,
yet our roots remain as one.

Unknown

It was January 7—Ukrainian Christmas. I call it that because we always celebrated two Christmases growing up: the traditional English one on December 25, which follows the Gregorian calendar (and happens to be my father's birthday); and the Ukrainian one on January 7, which aligns with the Julian calendar, where Epiphany is marked on January 6.

This year, with most of our extended family no longer nearby, it was just my children and me. We decided to do something we hadn't done in a long time and surprise my mother by going to church. Growing up, attending Mass was a regular Sunday ritual. The pews used to be full—family, friends, and members of our community. It is not the same anymore.

Today, the church feels quieter, emptier. I find myself wondering: Where have all the parishioners gone? It seems that the priority of attending Mass has faded, replaced by the busyness of modern life. Yet, there is still something grounding and sacred about being there, a reminder of our roots—and, perhaps, our resilience.

Of course, we were late. The weather was bad, and I had offered to pick up Larissa from her apartment, which added extra time to what would normally be a twenty-minute drive on a clear day. As I navigated the snow-covered roads, I noticed something different. My old self would have been anxious, irritated that we weren't arriving on time. But instead, I felt calm—grateful, even. I chose to be present, to enjoy the conversation unfolding around me. Listening to my children share their thoughts, their dreams, their bits of exciting news—I realized these were the moments that mattered. In a way, being late became a gift.

When we finally arrived, Larissa and her brother walked quietly into the church and immediately lit a beautiful candle for their brother, Danylo. It was a tender gesture, a silent act of remembrance that needed no words. Watching them, my heart swelled with both pride and sorrow—the kind that only comes from loving deeply and losing profoundly.

As they made their way down the side aisle, they spotted the nun who had once taught them catechism. Her face lit up in recognition and warmth. She was genuinely touched that they still remembered her after all these years. In her gentle way, she offered them some holy water to take home, as if handing them a piece of their faith, their history, something sacred to carry with them. During our lunch, Larissa was chatting with her brother Adrian and said, "Of course I remember going to church and seeing Sister Laurencia. Adrian, that's the church where my brothers and I were all christened."

As soon as I heard her say "*my brothers,*" my heart skipped a beat, and my eyes welled up with tears. I was so moved by how naturally she included Danylo in her recollection—as if time had folded in on itself and he was still right there beside them. In my mind, I whispered, *yes, your two brothers. Always your two brothers.*

It was such a tender moment—a beautiful reminder that Danylo is never truly gone or forgotten. He has a place in that church, just as he holds a permanent place in our hearts and lives.

Later that day, my mother began telling us a story about the tree that once stood in front of our childhood home. We gathered together on the couch, each of us cradling a glass of brandy, leaning in as another family memory began to unfold.

"You know, children, the *lypa*—the linden tree—is very symbolic for us," she began. "Back in Ukraine, we had a beautiful, large one on our front lawn. It seemed like every Ukrainian family had a *lypa* planted nearby. It is a special tree—one of healing, love, and hope."

She continued, "After we bought our house on Rosemont, Tato and I took the bus to a garden center to get a *lypa* for our own lawn. We didn't have a car then, so we waited until after the morning rush to set out on our mission. We found our tree—a strong, young *lypa*, about seven feet tall. We wrapped its trunk in a garbage bag and carried it to the bus stop.

"One bus passed us, then another, probably thinking, *'who are these crazy immigrants standing at a bus stop with a tree?'* But finally, a kind driver stopped to let us on. We carried the *lypa* on board—me at the front, Dido at the back—and rode all the way home. Luckily, it was midday, so the bus was nearly empty."

"Wow, you really did that, Baba?" Adrian exclaimed. "You brought a whole tree on the bus? It was that important?"

A simple bus ride might seem unusual to the kids now, but my mother's story captured their attention. What started as a practical task became a legacy. The *lypa* she and my father planted grew into something far greater than they could have imagined.

Intrigued, I later did some research of my own. As I'd suspected, there was a reason so many Ukrainian families planted *lypas* in their gardens. More than fifty years later, even though we've long since left that house, the linden tree still stands—tall, proud, and deeply rooted in our heritage.

Just last week, my mother and I had the joy of visiting that old home and sharing the story with the current owners. They had always wondered why the tree stood out, why it seemed to be the most prominent on the street. Now they knew: it was planted with love, adorned with quiet blessings, and infused with memory. Though I'd never considered the linden tree my personal symbol, I think differently now.

The linden holds deep meaning in Ukrainian and Eastern European culture. In ancient Slavic mythology, the *lypa* was considered sacred, often associated with deities of protection. Ukrainians have long chosen the linden as a symbol of resilience and unity, its presence in gardens reflecting both a connection to the land and to each other.

Beyond its beauty, the *lypa* is a healing tree—its blossoms used in teas known for their calming, restorative properties. Perhaps that's why, as a child, I always felt safe beneath its canopy, and why our home became a gathering place—for holidays, for grief, for joy.

In essence, the *lypa* represents love, memory, unity, and identity, deeply rooted in Ukrainian soil and spirit. Though we may be far from that place now, the linden tree in front of our old home still reaches skyward, a quiet testament to the hands that planted it, the stories it has witnessed, and the resilience it continues to embody. Even now, it casts a protective shade over the garden—just as it has over our family, and over Ukraine, through every storm and struggle.

Perhaps the trees we plant—and those planted long before us—do more than grow from the earth. Their roots live in us, nourishing the strength we carry and the branches we offer to others. Take a moment to feel the roots that live within you and notice how they guide the way you reach for the light.

REMEMBERING MY ANGEL

There is no footprint too small to leave an imprint on this world.
Unknown

November 11 rolls around again, as it does every year, and with it comes the most unforgettable day. It is the day we honor the courage of veterans, including those who continue to serve and fight for freedom today; and it is the day we honor the memory of my precious angel, Danylo, who left me over twenty-five years ago. Each year, I remember. And each year, the emotions creep up on me unexpectedly, catching me off guard. I cry, and then, as if by magic, symbols appear—reminders of his presence that I can't explain. "Hallelujah" softly plays on the radio, a white dove glides past my window, and I find myself drawn to the florist, purchasing a rose adorned with delicate babies' breath. I take it to the place where he was laid to rest in the serene beauty of Mount Royal cemetery.

Even though it's fall—the time when the flowers his older sister and younger brother plant for him, lose their leaves and wither—I know, deep within, that his life continues to live on in our souls. The seasons may change, but his memory remains timeless, unbroken.

I've often wondered: What if I were to take his picture and somehow age it, what would he look like now? And then I pause. Just as quickly as the thought comes, I somehow let it go. Deep down I know that Danylo is meant to be remembered just as he was—forever my baby.

Though Danylo will always be my deepest 'what if,' his presence is felt in the purest way—through a quiet strength that echoes in love, in memory, and in the spaces between each passing year.

I know these emotions will never fully fade and that they will always resurface, like waves that never cease, marking this day as both a sorrow and a tribute.

We have the strength to shed the tears,
The power to see through the darkness,
To light our faces with smiles,
And to be grateful.

This day reminds me to cherish every precious moment, to find resilience in love, and to recognize that we are held by those who came before us—by our angels.

I cannot undo what was done, nor bring back what was taken, but I do believe it all happened for a reason.

In remembrance and love,
For Danylo and all those who served,
Lest we forget.

As time passes, I've grown more spiritual, realizing that we each have a unique purpose in life. As long as we are alive, we continue to serve that purpose. Danylo's death has taught me to appreciate the angel I've been blessed with—an angel who sings in heaven and one I had the privilege of bringing into this world.

Each time a white bird flies past my window—something that happens almost daily now—I feel not just his spirit, but a deep sense of peace, freedom, and love. It brings joy to my heart and pulls me forward, pushing me to do more with my life because I know he is guiding me.

The angels were the shield I created growing up, protecting me from harm. They've always been with me, offering guidance when needed. Now, more than ever, I trust them. I embrace the idea that Danylo is always with me. Angels can only bring good into our lives—good energy—and perhaps that is why I avoid negative energy at all costs. I cannot stand confrontation, and when I sense it, I walk away. I refuse to stay in that space.

The angels give me power—or perhaps it's the power I've always had, a power I've now remembered. I am a free-spirited woman, a survivor, a believer, a thriver—a magnet for positive change. A luminary. With the guidance of angels, I feel an unshakable strength, a force unbound by the physical limitations of the body. I draw from them, from the purity and clarity they offer, to do the work I'm meant to do. The power I now embrace is more than just mine; it is a force that flows through me, amplified by the wisdom and energy of those who have transcended this earth.

In my daily practice, I am reminded of their presence through a ritual that has become my anchor. Each morning, I select one or two angel cards—gifts from my dear friend, Enza, an angel in my life since 2004. With each card, I do a reading, and journal on its message. It is a way for me to connect with the angels and invite their guidance into my day. It's as if the angels surround me—physically, through the cards, and spiritually, through the messages they impart. These cards remind me that I am not alone, and with each reading, I feel the presence of something greater, something divine, gently nudging me toward my path.

Take a moment to ask yourself: What do I want my power to be?

Because you too have power. We all do.

What I've learned is that hope and gratitude are the keys to a happy, healthy life. Despite all the losses and struggles, they've kept me going, alive and striving for a better tomorrow. If my grandmother could see the life her daughter created for her family, she would be proud, knowing it was all built on love, care, and gratitude.

I carry that legacy with me—strength and resilience passed down through generations and now to my daughter. The book my mother was meant to write is being written through me. The bond of family, the thread of our ancestors, remains alive, permeating through time.

No matter what the world becomes, we will persevere—not without struggle or sorrow—but always with hope and gratitude. That is how you do life.

Bringing Light to Loss: Redefining grief to reclaim hope and meaning teaches us that even in our most profound grief, there is room for light, growth, and transformation. I've often wondered why I dislike the word 'grief.' Even before experiencing it in its hardest form, I found the sound and meaning of the word unsettling. But today, I choose to redefine grief in a way that fosters growth, a way that lets me find light and meaning in the midst of loss.

GRIEF
Gratitude
Reminds us of the
Invaluable
Essence from which growth
Flourishes.

This is how I choose to embrace the word GRIEF—not in denial, but in hope.

Now, when I think of grief, I no longer see only loss. I see the light that comes with growth, the hope and gratitude that lead to transformation. And you can find this too.

As Norman Cousins reminds us "the greatest loss in life is not death itself, but what dies inside of us while we are still alive"—and we have the power to revive it.

Within each of us lies a spark that adversity tries to dim—a spark of hope, love, and purpose. No matter how lost or broken we feel, we possess the strength to rekindle that light. Let this story be a reminder that even in our darkest moments, we can choose to heal, grow, and rediscover the parts of ourselves that once felt forgotten. Our resilience is our greatest inheritance, and the legacy we leave behind is built by every moment we dare to revive what once seemed lost.

In this moment of reflection, ask yourself: What part of me have I left behind that I am ready to revive?

Let this be your moment to reignite your passions, reclaim your dreams, and nurture the light within you. Your future self will thank you.

A LEGACY OF HOPE

The meaning of life is to find your gift.
The purpose of life is to give it away.
Pablo Picasso

As I reach the end of this book, I am filled with gratitude—not only for the healing and lessons that have unfolded throughout this journey but also for the opportunity to share it with you, the reader. I am deeply thankful that you have chosen to be a part of this movement—helping others on their grief journey and honoring the 'Child Life' program. This story, woven with personal tragedy and resilience, is one of transformation. It stands as a testament to the strength that lies within us all, even in the darkest of times.

But my hope for you doesn't end with these pages. It is my deepest wish that the insights, tools, and stories shared throughout this book will not only reside in your mind but also ignite something profound in your heart.

1. I have learned that the death of my son does not define me, nor does it make me a victim.
2. In the face of loss, we always have a choice—to remain stuck in grief or to rise above it. We can choose healing, hope, and ultimately, freedom. My own transformation, from the depths of despair to reclaiming joy and a renewed sense of purpose, proves

that no matter how great the pain, there is always potential for something beautiful to emerge.

3. Pain can be transformed through acceptance, gratitude, and deliberate action.

4. Suffering is optional when we take control of our healing through faith and intention.

5. Generational patterns may shape our experiences, but we can break free from them.

6. Love and loss are intertwined: where there is love, there is loss— and the capacity to heal.

7. Grief is individual. Pace it in the way that best serves you. Healing is not linear, and it is okay to take your own time and space to process it.

8. Make a decision to change, and do one small thing toward it. Every small step taken toward healing counts. It is all about progress, not perfection.

9. Do not lose sight of who you are—remain true to you. Even in the midst of loss, you have the power to stay connected to your essence and the things that bring you joy.

10. You belong to you, and no one else. Honor that. Be you, always. The most important relationship you have is with yourself. Nurture it with love, respect, and kindness.

As long as there is life, you have the power to choose how to live it. May these words remind you that healing is possible, growth is inevitable, and the path forward is yours to shape.

I choose to live my life with gratitude and abundance, knowing that tomorrow is promised to no-one. I raise my hand to you for all that you have lived, and all that is still to come.

Looking up at the sky with a smile, my heart overflows.
I carry my million-dollar family in my soul,
and the love that began with one small heartbeat
continues to echo through everything I do.

This is not an ending;
just a quiet turning of the page,
where love lives on,
and hope writes the next line.

I carry him with me
in every step, every breath,
every silent moment where love speaks louder than words.

As I close this chapter,
I leave you with a piece of my heart 🩶
a poem written for my son,
my angel, my strength.

DANYLO: MY STRENGTH, MY REASON

What we have once enjoyed we can never lose.
All that we love deeply becomes a part of us.
Helen Keller

Strength
One syllable, eight letters, a powerful word.
Is it something we learn?
Is it already within?
Graced by the Good Lord at birth
To help us endure whatever shows up
To find the blessings and lessons that it contains
To see the light in the dark moments
Because there are…
Things may look heavy and bleak now
But faith will restore the trust
A new door will open
For it is how we see the world, and how protected we feel
Surrounded by a higher being

By our loved ones that have left us behind
Leaving an overwhelming void in our hearts…
But the daily reminders of their presence remain in our existence
And that is what keeps us going
For we cannot undo what was done,
Or bring back what was taken,
But believe it all happened for a reason
We have the strength to shed the tears
We have the power to see through the darkness
To illuminate our faces with smiles
And be grateful
Be strong,
Be courageous
Because, we are not alone
He will always be with me; he will not fail nor forsake me.
He is my strength.

THE END

Nurturing Your Journey: Ways to Feel, Heal, and Rise

As we've walked together through the pages of this book, I want to offer you gentle ways to continue nurturing your path toward healing, hope, and growth. If the message here has touched your heart and stirred something within you, these next steps can support you as you keep moving forward:

Share the Message

- **Create a book club**: Let's keep this important conversation going. If you're starting a book club, I'd be honored to join your discussions and explore together the themes of healing, hope, and transformation.
- **Invite me to speak:** If you're part of a community, association, or organization, I'd love the opportunity to speak at your next event. Whether the topic is overcoming loss, navigating personal transformation, or living authentically, I can tailor my message to inspire and support your group in taking meaningful steps forward. To book a call or learn more, please visit **taniachomyk.com**.

Deepen your Growth

- **Support for groups**: If you're part of a group or organization navigating grief, career transitions, or seeking clarity and empowerment, I offer resources, guidance, and consultation to help your group move forward with intention and healing.
- **Be the CEO of Your Career/Life Program**: This eight-week journey is designed to help you reclaim your power, align with your true self, and lead your life with purpose and passion. If you're ready to step fully into your potential, this program awaits you.

Join a Community of Empowerment

- **Empower Her Summit**: What started as a vision last fall has blossomed into a reality: a vibrant space for women to be seen, heard, and valued. Mark your calendar for October 5, 2025, and join us to Rise-Lead-Thrive together. Learn more at **empowerhersummit.ca**.

RESOURCES THAT SUPPORTED MY JOURNEY

There are a few treasures that have gently carried me along the way:

Kyle Gray's *Angel Prayers Oracle Cards* have become a daily ritual, filling my mornings with warmth, reassurance, and a sense of divine guidance.

If you have a story to share—one that could inspire, uplift, or help others—here are two incredible resources that helped me in my journey:

- **Speaker Slam (Toronto, Ontario):** If you're looking to refine your message and bring your story to life on stage, Speaker Slam provides expert coaching, training, and guidance to help you craft and deliver impactful talks with confidence.
- **The Awakened School (Colorado):** For those seeking deeper spiritual guidance in their writing journey, The Awakened School offers transformative programs that help you connect with your purpose, find your authentic voice, and share your message from a place of alignment and truth.

For more information about my work, upcoming events, and ways we can journey together, please visit **taniachomyk.com**.

Together, let's build a legacy of hope—not just for ourselves, but also for those who will follow. No matter what the challenges, faith can light the way, and hope can carry us forward. Your journey is unique, and every step you take to feel, heal, and rise brings you closer to the life you are meant to live.

APPENDICES:
HEAR MY VOICE

To accompany the stories and insights shared in this book, I invite you to watch any of my speeches that hold a special place in my heart:

- **The Light Within the Underdog**, Speaker Slam, July 15, 2022 LuLa Lounge Toronto, Ontario
  https://www.youtube.com/watch?v=TPvwNxs2TXU
- **The Journey:** Grand Slam Speech, November 2022, performed at CBC Glenn Gould Theatre.
  https://www.youtube.com/watch?v=sx_daFjKgG4
- **The Million-Dollar Family:** Award-winning speech, June 2022.
  https://www.youtube.com/watch?v=x5E-mwTrCW0

These speeches reflect my personal journey and the themes of healing, hope, and resilience that I carry with me every day. May they inspire you as you continue your own path forward.

REFERENCES: BIBLIOGRAPHY

Anderson, J.W. *Angels We Have Heard on High: A Book of Seasonal Blessings* (The Angel Press, 1997)

Brown, B. (2015). *Rising strong: How the ability to reset transforms the way we live, love, parent, and lead.* Spiegel & Grau.

Cuddy, Amy. *Presence: Bringing Your Boldest Self to Your Biggest Challenges* (Little, Brown and Company, 2015)

Dickinson, A. (2014). *Reinvention: Changing your life, your career, your future.* Penguin Canada.

Eurich, T. (2017). *Insight: The surprising truth about how others see us, how we see ourselves, and why the answers matter more than we think.* Crown Publishing Group.

Fields, J. (2021). *Sparked: Discover your unique imprint for work that makes you come alive.* Sparked Press.

Konovalov, O. (2019). *The vision code: How to create and execute a compelling vision for your business.* Wiley Press.

Kübler-Ross, E. (1969). *On death and dying.* Macmillan.

Kushner, H.S. (2004). *When bad things happen to good people.* Anchor Books.

Menakem, R. (2017). *My grandmother's hands: Racialized trauma and the pathway to mending our hearts and bodies*. Central Recovery Press.

Patwell, B., & Seashore, E. (2019). *Triple impact coaching: Use the 3 powers to maximize your coaching effectiveness*. Coaching Out of the Box.

Quinn, G. (2001). *May the angels be with you: A psychic helps you find your spirit guides and your true purpose*.

Stanier, M.B. (2016). *The coaching habit: Say less, ask more & change the way you lead forever*. Box of Crayons Press.

Wu, C., Odden, M. C., Fisher, G. G., Stawski, R. S., & Stoddard, S. A. (2016). Association of retirement age with mortality: A population-based longitudinal study among older adults in the USA. *Journal of Epidemiology & Community Health*, 70(9), 917–923. https://doi.org/10.1136/jech-2015-207097

ACKNOWLEDGEMENTS

I would like to begin by offering my deepest gratitude to my children, Larissa and Adrian. You are my angels on Earth, inspiring me each and every day. Larissa, you were my rock during the most difficult moments of my life. Your strength, compassion, and love carried me when I could barely stand. Adrian, you are the angel that arrived when I needed you most. Your spirit brought a light into my life that I never knew I needed, and for that, I will be forever grateful.

A special thank you to my dearest mother, who continues to show me the true meaning of strength and grace at the tender age of ninety-one. Your resilience and love have shaped me into who I am today, and for that, I am forever grateful. I also want to honor my great-grandmother, Tetiana, whose legacy of resilience, strength, and the fight for freedom lives on in me and in the generations of Ukrainian women before and after her.

To my dearest sister Lida and brother Zenon, and families, thank you for your unwavering support, love, and understanding. You have been there through every high and low, never questioning my path or my need for healing.

To my partner Ken, and friends, thank you for your support, words of encouragement, and belief in me. Your wisdom and love have been integral in my healing and writing journey.

I am deeply grateful to the many people who have come into my life, each of you playing a part in my healing and my ability to share my story. The organizations and communities I have been a part of, including those that allowed me to speak, write, and share my journey with the world, have all provided a space for me to step into my truth. You have helped me transform pain into purpose, and for that, I am eternally thankful.

A special thank you to those who helped bring this book to life (Rachael Jayne & Datta Groover)—text editors, Deborah Murell and Kim Wiesenberger; beta readers and reviewers, Beverley Patwell, Iryna Melnyk, Antonella Nizolla, Tam Nguyen, Luvana DiFrancesco, Enza DeMartinis, Rina Rovinelli, Carla Marrouche, Gerald l'Ecuyer, Antonio Bernardelli, and Anna Manocchio; fellow coaches and colleagues who supported me; and to the readers and listeners who've shared their own stories. This book is not just my own, it is the result of a collective effort, and I am humbled by the love and care that has gone into it.

Lastly, I would like to acknowledge my angel, Danylo, whose spirit guides me every day. Though I can no longer hold him, I feel him with me in every step I take, every word I write, and every part of this journey.

Thank you to all who have been a part of this journey—your presence in my life means more than words can express.

ABOUT THE AUTHOR

Tania Chomyk is a life transition expert, award-winning resilience speaker, and grief educator. With over thirty years of experience in education, career development, and personal growth, she helps people move through life's toughest moments with clarity, courage, and compassion. Based in Montreal, she brings a 'can-do' attitude to transforming life's challenges into opportunities. As the creator of the 'Be the CEO of Your Career and Life' program and the Empower Her Summit, Tania helps individuals build clarity, confidence, and control over their professional and personal journeys, inspiring them to lead with heart and live with purpose.

www.ingramcontent.com/pod-product-compliance
Lightning Source LLC
Chambersburg PA
CBHW021142130626
46554CB00005B/1625